Carnegie Endowment for International Peace

DIVISION OF INTERCOURSE AND EDUCATION

Publication No. 1

SOME ROADS TOWARDS PEACE

A Report to the Trustees of the Endowment

On Observations Made in China and Japan in 1912

BY

CHARLES W. ELIOT

PUBLISHED BY THE ENDOWMENT
WASHINGTON, D. C.
1914

COPYRIGHT 1913
BY THE
CARNEGIE ENDOWMENT FOR INTERNATIONAL PEACE,
WASHINGTON, D. C.

PRESS OF BYRON S. ADAMS,
WASHINGTON, D. C.

PREFACE

The report which follows is the result of a journey to the East undertaken by Mr. Charles W. Eliot in pursuance of a definite plan adopted by the Trustees of the Carnegie Endowment for International Peace. This plan includes frequent international visits by representative men for the purpose of explaining the object and plans of work of the Endowment and of ascertaining in what practical ways the Endowment may helpfully exercise its influence in various parts of the world. It is also the belief of the Trustees that through such international visits by representative men the various civilized peoples will come to know and to understand each other better, to see more clearly each other's point of view and so to diminish the opportunities for misunderstanding and international conflict.

The journey of Mr. Eliot to China and to Japan does not stand alone. Mr. Hamilton W. Mabie spent more than six months of the year 1912–1913 in Japan and Mr. Robert Bacon has recently spent three months in some of the capital cities of South America. During the year 1911–1912 Professor Nitobe, an eminent educator of Japan, spent eight months in the United States, and at the present time Professor Shosuke Sato is visiting a number of American universities and agricultural colleges. Between European countries similar visits are also being carried on, and in the course of one of these Baron d'Estournelles de Constant has recently made an important and widely discussed address at Nuremberg.

It is the purpose of the Trustees of the Carnegie Endowment to follow these visits with such other forms of activity as may seem wise and practicable. Already as a consequence of Mr. Eliot's visit to China, Professor Frank J. Goodnow of Columbia University is in residence at Peking as the legal adviser of the government of the Republic of China in all matters relating to constitutional and administrative law. The helping hand of the Endowment is in this way stretched half round the world in order to assist in a constructive piece of nation building, and so to contribute to national stability and international peace.

NICHOLAS MURRAY BUTLER,
Acting Director.

January 2, 1914

CONTENTS.

	Page
Introduction	1
The Superintendence of Eastern Peoples by Western Powers	3
Universal Education	5
The Introduction of Western Medicine and Public Sanitation	6
The Regulation of Migrations of Laborers	7
Racial Mixtures	8
The Insecurity of Property Under Despotic Governments	9
Liberty of Association and Incorporation	10
The Administration of Justice	11
The Regulation of the Vices	12
Comparative Legislation in Western Dependencies in the Far East	13
The Causes of War Have Changed	13
The Future Causes of War	14
The Fear of Invasion	16
The Exemption of Private Property From Capture at Sea	17
The Occidental Desire for Ports, Concessions, and Spheres of Influence in the East	17
Alien Government	18
The Revolution in China	19
The Physical and Moral Qualities of the Chinese	21
The Chinese Have No Knowledge of Western Medicine	21
The Missionary Medical Services	22
The Manchus Gone Forever	23
The Imperial Maritime Customs Service	23
The Manchu Empire Had No Proper Revenues	24
Two Useful Institutions at Shanghai	25
Education Among the Chinese	26
The Transformation of Chinese Education	27
Influence of Mission Schools and Colleges on Chinese Education	28
Changes in Chinese Education Essential to National Unity	29
Travelling Fellowships for Chinese Graduates	29
The Protestant Missions in China	30
The Difficulties of the Provisional Government	32
The Sentiments Which Make for Chinese Unity	33
A Strong National Government to be the Work of Many Years	34
The Value of the Chinese Markets	35
An American Free Public Library at Peking	36
The Six Powers Loan to China	38
The Conditions of Successful Borrowing by China	39

CONTENTS—*Continued*.

	Page
The Selection of Foreign Experts	41
The Pure Race is the Best	42
Just Sympathy With the Revolution	42
A Glimpse of Korea	45
The Relations Between Japan and the United States	46
Japanese Courtesy	47
From Fusan to Tokyo	48
The Japanese System of Public Instruction	49
Uniform Programs Well Enforced Lead to a Uniform or Averaged Product	50
The Liberalizing Influence of Endowed Institutions	50
Sense Training in Japanese Schools	51
The Education of Women in Japan	51
Effects of the Factory System in Japan	52
Japanese Temples and Shrines	53
The Maintenance of Religious Observances	54
The Toleration of All Religions in Japan	55
Industrial Changes—Business Morality	56
Medical Science and Art in Japan	57
The Desires and Ambitions of the Japanese	58
The Domination of the Pacific	59
International Peace is the Interest of Japan	59
Japanese Labor and Capital Needed at Home	60
Appropriate Expenditures of Carnegie Endowment Income in Japan	61
The Schools in Hawaii	62
Hawaiian Experience in Crossing Races	63
The Labor Problem in Hawaii—Immigration and Importation	64
Profitable Expenditures for the Promotion of Peace	65
Appendix I	67
The International Institute of China	67
Letter of Dr. Charles W. Eliot	67
Letter of Rev. Gilbert Reid, Director	68
Appendix II	70
Memorial for the Endowment of a Hospital in China	70
Appendix III	73
Memorial for the Endowment of a Free Public Library in Peking, China	73
Appendix IV	76
Letter of Dr. Charles W. Eliot to Hon. Tong Shao-yi	76
Appendix V	79
An International Hospital for Tokyo	79
Appendix VI	87
Abstract of a Memorandum on the Subject of the Education of the Children of Foreigners Resident in the Far East	87

SOME ROADS TOWARDS PEACE

A Report

On Observations Made in China and Japan in 1912

To the Trustees of the Carnegie
   Endowment for International Peace:

In accordance with instructions received, under date of October 30, 1911, from your Division of Intercourse and Education through President Nicholas Murray Butler, Acting Director of the Division, I travelled round the world in the period between November 7, 1911, when I sailed from New York, and August 10, 1912, when I reached Boston overland from San Francisco, going as quickly as possible from New York to Colombo, and returning home from Honolulu by the shortest route without stopping on the way. My time for observation and study, with the exception of a single week in Hawaii, was spent wholly in the Far East, between December 2, 1911, the date of my arrival at Colombo, and July 13, 1912, when I left Yokohama.

A resolution adopted by the Executive Committee on October 26, 1911, stated that the proposed journey was to be made "to Asia in the interest of the work of the Division of Intercourse and Education and that of the Endowment as a whole." Dr. Butler as Acting Director further informed me that "It is the desire of the Committee that you should, at your own convenience and in such ways as seem to you appropriate, explain in the various countries of Asia that you will visit, the organization and purposes of the Endowment and its plans so far as now outlined; that you will study the public opinion of the several Asiatic peoples, particularly as relates to questions of international significance; and that you will procure material for a report to the Trustees through the Division of Intercourse and Education, as to what activities may wisely and helpfully be planned in and for the Asiatic countries that will advance the cause of peace and international good will."

With the exception of about a month during which I was incapacitated by an operation for appendicitis in Kandy, Ceylon, I was able to apply myself diligently to the work outlined in the resolution and letter above quoted. Among the methods I used the most important was conversation with educated natives of the countries I visited, who had succeeded in business, or a profession, or public service, and with foreigners resident in the East, such as diplomats, consuls, merchants, teachers, missionaries, and public administrators. I also made numerous addresses at schools, colleges, and universities, at some churches, missions, and establishments of the Young Men's Christian Asociation, and before societies organized to promote international peace and good will. I had many opportunities of addressing small companies of gentlemen, or of ladies and gentlemen, at luncheons and dinners, sometimes at private houses, and sometimes in public rooms. For my own instruction, the private conversations were more advantageous that any other contacts. In Ceylon, China, and Japan I met many native ladies and gentlemen who could speak English; but even when an interpreter was necessary the conversations were more fruitful than any other form of intercourse.

In China and Japan it was a necessary part of my work to make public addresses; but one who cannot speak Chinese or Japanese is always at a grave disadvantage in addressing Chinese or Japanese audiences, however cultivated. A large part of his audience will be unable to understand English; and even if an interpreter is employed, it is doubtful if the interpretation, however prompt and skilful, will give a thoroughly correct idea of the speaker's utterances. In many cases I was assured by listeners who understood both English and Chinese or Japanese that my meaning had not been perfectly conveyed to the native audience. Moreover, hasty versions or summaries of speeches in English made for the local newspapers are inevitably even more inaccurate than those ordinarily made in the United States by reporters who can only write longhand. These difficulties will always attend the use of a lecture method by English-speaking lecturers in either China or Japan; and yet English is far the best European language in which to attempt communication with Orientals. For this reason the Western mind will, in general, get better access to the Oriental mind through print than through speech,—through books, periodicals, and newspapers in the Western languages, and through carefully prepared translations of Western writings into Chinese and Japanese. This principle, of course, does not apply to highly educated Orientals who understand English, nor to intercourse through conversation in which address and personal quality tell.

Through letters of introduction, and the good offices of American and English friends long resident in China and Japan, and of Chinese and Japanese graduates of American universities, and particularly of Harvard university, I had access to many leaders of opinion and public servants in both countries, but to more in Japan than in China, because many Japanese students have graduated at Harvard University during the past forty years, a large proportion of whom have attained high station in their native country. On this account, I was given during my thirty days in Japan every facility for seeing what I wished to see, and meeting the persons I desired to meet. Since many of the conversations I was privileged to have were of an intimate and confidential character, relating to living persons, to policies and states of opinion not publicly announced, and to political and industrial methods not yet fully worked out, I deem it best to omit throughout the following report, with a few exceptions, names of persons and places, asking the Trustees to accept the sentiments and opinions expressed in the report—so far as they are acceptable—on grounds of probability and verisimilitude, or of plain inherent truth.

A few passages in the report relate to the Second and Third Divisions of the work of the Endowment as now planned, namely, to that of Economics and that of International Law, but all the recommendations for future action on the part of the Trustees relate, as is fitting, to the Division of Intercourse and Education, from which my commission proceeded.

The Superintendence of Eastern Peoples by Western Powers

It was well that the route adopted for my journey took me first to Oriental countries which are under the control or supervision of Western powers. I had never before been in the Far East, although I had visited the near East, as it can be seen in north Africa, Constantinople, and Egypt. I had never before seen so clearly the conditions under which different Oriental races have lived beside each other on the same territory for centuries with but little racial admixture, or the conditions under which religions so different as the Mohammedan, the Buddhist, and the Christian may coexist on the same soil indefinitely without open strife. I had never before seen migrations of laborers on a large scale induced by capital, unopposed by government, regulated, though imperfectly, by government, and causing grave social and industrial evils, while making possible, or promoting, profitable industries.

Throughout British, French, and Netherlands India, the spoliation of the native populations, in the direct interest of the superintending governments or peoples, has nearly ceased; but the present theory of Western control requires that the controlled peoples shall pay, as a rule, the costs of governing them; so that the limit of expenditure for promoting the welfare of any such people is that proportion of the public revenue derived from that people which can be applied to welfare work, like medical service, sanitation, irrigation, or education. If the supply of schools, dispensaries, and hospitals in any region superintended by a Western power is scanty, it is because the public revenue from that region is inadequate to meet those desirable expenditures, after other needs, held to be more pressing, have been duly provided for. If much-needed public works are executed slowly and incompletely, it is because the return from taxes is not adequate to pay for quick and thorough work. Hence, the civilizing processes which diminish the burdens of ignorance and misery, and make for order, comfort, and peace, are introduced and carried forward in the superintended Eastern countries with a slowness which astonishes and mortifies a fresh impartial observer from the West, but seems quite natural and proper to the old foreign resident, or to the commercial adventurer who is seeking an immediately profitable investment.

With some occasional exceptions, the policy of the Western governments which control Oriental populations seems to be nowadays intelligently directed to the promotion of the material well-being of the subject peoples, although not evenly in the different possessions or colonies. The more prosperous an Oriental people becomes, the better market it can afford to Occidental manufacturers. The Western powers now see clearly their interest in increasing the purchasing power of Oriental consumers by the million. In developing Oriental self-respect with the associated virtue of self-control, Western policy has been less successful; but in this regard there are clear signs of improvement in the prevailing sentiments and opinions of the several European governments and peoples which are exercising control over Oriental peoples. The fundamental object of Western colonization, or other form of occupation in the East, is, as it always has been, the extension of European trade and the increase of European wealth; but the opinion is beginning to prevail extensively in Europe and among Europeans who live in the East, that these objects can best be accomplished by increasing the intelligence, skill, and well-being of the Eastern populations controlled, by raising their standards of living, relieving them from superstitious terrors, social bondages, and industrial handicaps, and by creating among them new wants and ambitions.

The principal means to these worthy ends are (a) education both elementary and advanced, and particularly the instruction of young people in the fundamental trades, and of adult cultivators in the best methods of producing the chief crops of each country, and in the expediency of cultivating a variety of crops; (b) preventive medicine and an effective public health organization directed to the relief of current suffering, the prevention of sweeping pestilences, and the increase of industrial efficiency; (c) sound legislation concerning migratory labor, and the means of securing for large-scale industries an adequate supply of trustworthy laborers; (d) the levying of taxes under public law, the collection of taxes by honest salaried officials, and the publication of national budgets; (e) liberty of association and incorporation with limited liability for commercial, industrial, educational, religious and charitable objects; (f) courts and an administration of justice which command public confidence; and (g) effective regulations concerning opium, alcohol, gambling, and prostitution. All these means may be provided through the sole action of the superintending alien government, or by a combination of powers created by the superintending government and exercised by the government and the superintended population acting together. Their successful action depends on the maintenance throughout the superintended territory of public order, and of racial and religious toleration. Every one of these means, well used, tends strongly though indirectly towards sound and just national conditions, and hence towards orderly and reasonable international conduct.

Each of these means of enlightenment and progress needs some further elucidation.

Universal Education

(a) If we except the extraordinary instance of Japan, popular education has only lately begun to work among the Oriental peoples. Its object is not only to increase the intelligence of the people as a whole, but also to relieve them from the many terrors contained in the popular religious beliefs, and from the bondage of superstitious social and industrial habits, and particularly from the extraordinary restrictions imposed by caste. The wonderful success the government of Japan has attained in providing the means of universal elementary education and of the higher education for a numerous class selected for merit and capacity, has stimulated all the Oriental peoples to desire free public instruction; but the superintending Western governments have thus far met this desire for instruction in only an imperfect way, and to a limited extent. In India the expenditures of the government on education began at the top, and have not been followed by adequate expenditure at the bottom; and throughout that portion of the Far East which is superintended by Western powers the expenditure on public education has been far too small. Yet it is only through widespread education, open through all its grades to deserving and capable youth, that the population at large can be made more intelligent and skilful, and more capable of true progress, social, industrial, and governmental. To promote sound education in the East by giving information about Western educational institutions, methods, and results, by founding international scholarships and lectureships, and by establishing free libraries on the American type, would be a sure way to increase the mutual acquaintance of East and West, and to develop mutual good will.

In the field of education there is one specific gift which the West can make to the East that would gradually produce a great change in the working of the Oriental mind. The Oriental has been a student of the abstract. He has proceeded by intuition and meditation, and has accepted his philosophy and his religion largely from authorities. He has never practised the inductive philosophy, and to this day knows very little about it—except of course recently in Japan. The West, which owes its astonishing progress within the last four hundred years chiefly to the inductive method of ascertaining truth, can impart to the East a knowledge of that method by showing the Eastern peoples how to teach the natural and physical sciences in schools of all grades, in such a way as to train in children and youth the powers of observation and the capacity for making an exact record of the facts, and then drawing the just, limited inference from the facts observed and compared. The best way to withdraw the Oriental mind in part from the region of literary imagination and speculative philosophy which is congenial to it, and to give it the means of making independent progress in the region of fact and truth, is to teach science, agriculture, trades, and economics in all Eastern schools by the experimental, laboratory method which within fifty years has come into vogue among the Western peoples. Commercial, industrial, and social reform would be greatly promoted by the diffusion of such instruction among the rising generation. Such instruction, actively carried on for fifty years throughout the Eastern world, would modify profoundly the main differences between the working of the Occidental and the Oriental mind. Even the religious conceptions of the East would be favorably modified by the adoption there of the inductive method, just as that method has modified organized Christianity in the West. No international intercourse could possibly be more truly beneficent than this imparting of the inductive philosophy to India and China, and all the intervening countries. Japan has already mastered it, to her immense advantage.

The Introduction of Western Medicine and Public Sanitation

(b) To increase industrial efficiency and steady productiveness throughout the Oriental countries, it is indispensable that the practice of Western medicine and surgery and of public sanitation should be everywhere introduced. The working efficiency of some of the populations is now diminished to a formidable degree by the chronic prevalence among them of preventable and curable diseases, and by the occasional destructive pestilences which sweep unchecked through the Oriental communities, and kill many thousands of men, women, and children before their time. In southern India and many other parts of the East the hookworm disease presses heavily on the agricultural population; but government makes little or no effort either to cure the present victims, or to prevent the continuous development of this disease. Only in Japan is effective resistance made to the always recurring pestilences; and even there tuberculosis, leprosy, and other ever-present diseases go imperfectly controlled. Whether we look at disease and premature death as sources of heavy industrial losses, or as preventable causes of grievous human suffering, we find the gift of Western medicine and surgery to the Oriental populations to be one of the most precious things that Western civilization can do for the East. To spread through the East the knowledge of Western medicine and sanitation by building and conducting good hospitals, dispensaries, and laboratories for medical diagnosis, establishing boards of health, and providing defenses against plague, cholera, smallpox, and tuberculosis, is the surest way to persuade intelligent people in the East that they may expect much good from the inductive philosophy of the West acting in combination with the Christian religion in its simplest forms. There is no better subject than medicine in which to teach the universal inductive method.

The Regulation of Migrations of Laborers

(c) In order to its profitable use, the Western capital planted in Eastern soil and in Eastern mines, factories, and transportation companies, is almost always in urgent need of considerable amounts of trustworthy human labor; and such labor it is often impossible to procure at the places where the capital is planted, because the local native population has not been in the habit of doing steady work, does not like it, and does not need it for the support of a family in the accustomed way. Hence, promoted or induced migrations of laborers, often under unjust and unwholesome conditions. Such migrations have been, and still are, in the East sources of serious irritation and unfriendly feeling among the different colonies of Western powers, and between China and several of those colonies, possessions, or "spheres of influence." The regulation of emigration and immigration should be the object of anxious care with all the Oriental governments, whether alien or native; and great pains should be taken to prevent emigrants from leaving their own country under conditions that will probably involve them in serious moral and physical deterioration, and economic loss. Wherever large bodies of unmarried men emigrate to a strange land in search of work under conditions imperfectly known to them, the chances are that they will live in barracks on isolated plantations, or near isolated mines or factories, and that family life will be impossible for them. Under such circumstances laborers degenerate rapidly both morally and physically, and out of their wretchedness come intercolonial, international, and interracial disputes. It would be a very great improvement in the regulation of the migrations of laboring people now going on in many parts of the world and on a large scale, if the migration of large numbers of unmarried men, without women, could be prevented or restricted. The desirable immigrant is the healthy, strong man who comes to the new land with wife and children, meaning to settle there for good. All laws against "contract" labor impede family immigration; because a prudent head of a family wants to know before he starts from home where he is to earn his family's livelihood in the new land.

All sorts of experiments in imported labor have been tried in the Orient, and particularly in the British possessions there. The cost of importing the laborers has been borne sometimes by the planters or other capitalists who desired more laborers, and sometimes by the planters and the government; and sometimes the cost of importation has been paid by the planter, and charged by him to the imported laborer as a debt to be repaid by deductions from his future wages. On the accounts of some Western incorporated companies working in the East these "coolie debts" have even been carried as an asset of the corporation. In many cases of importation very little attention has been paid to keeping the imported laborer healthy and contented. He has often been lodged badly and fed poorly, and very little attention has been paid to his health, or to his need of family life and of reasonable recreations. The most successful method of importation involves domiciling the laborer in a cottage, with a piece of land which he may call his own. It may almost be said that in the East the only imported laborer who is worth importing is the one who has the home-making instinct, who has no intention of returning to his former country, and can be held by home ties to the land on which he has once settled. Wandering and shifting laborers will not answer the needs of capital throughout the East; and they are sure to be a cause of irritation and ultimate loss to both the community which sends them forth, and that to which they resort. The valuable immigrant has left home to better his condition. If he does not better it, his sacrifice has proved a failure, his example will not be followed, and he himself will never be a satisfactory laborer in his new field. The cottage immigrant is the desirable immigrant, no matter what his race. The unmarried barracks immigrant is always undesirable, unless he is an enterprising youngster with means to try a rash adventure, or comes for a short period with the intent to return to his native country,—just as Italian laborers by thousands resort to Switzerland and southern Germany for temporary employment in quarrying, stone laying, digging, and tunneling, intending to return in a few months to their native land.

The regulation of immigration all over the world is in an unsatisfactory condition. Positive regulations exist which are both unnecessary and unjust, and desirable regulations have been omitted; because it has not been clearly perceived that the only way to increase the number of settled laborers in any country which lacks an adequate working force, is to make the imported laborers contented in their new field by securing for them family life under favorable conditions, healthy surroundings, and the pleasures or recreations to which they are accustomed. It must be made not only the pecuniary interest of the imported laborer to remain in his new field. His surroundings and his tasks must be more favorable to his contentment than anything in his former experience; and he must see a better outlook for his children than any his native country offered. Under such conditions the emigration of hundreds of thousands of persons from a country where they were not well off to another country where they are better off and can be made highly useful, would no longer be a source of irritation and hard feeling between nations; and capital would obtain an adequate supply of trustworthy labor just where it was most needed.

Racial Mixtures

The difficulties about immigration have been much aggravated by misconceptions and misunderstandings about racial mixtures. The experience of the East teaches that the intermarriage of races which are distinctly unlike is undesirable; because the progeny from such mixtures is, as a rule, inferior to each of the parent stocks, both physically and morally, a fact which has been demonstrated on a large scale. The Eurasians throughout the East are regarded with disfavor alike by Europeans and Asiatics; and the successive generations of Eurasians show rapid degeneracy, unless they revert soon to one or other of the parent stocks. All through the East diverse races have lived for centuries side by side on the same territory without mixing, except to an insignificant degree, and even that the result of vice. The notion that strong races have been produced, or are to be produced, by a blend, or amalgam, of many different races, gets no support from Oriental experience. Races which are really kindred may safely intermarry; but races conspicuously distinct cannot. The centuries-long distinctness of different races inhabiting the same territory in the far East has doubtless been promoted or maintained in part by the differences of religion which there exist, and in India by the caste system; but different races which have embraced the same religion have continued distinct in many parts of the Orient for long periods of time, though living side by side on the same soil. The immigration question, therefore, need not be complicated by any racial problem, provided that each of several races abiding in the same territory keeps itself pure, as the Japanese do wherever they live.

To mitigate the grievances created by the immigration question, or to prevent the occurrence of such grievances, would be a good way to secure the maintenance of friendly relations between any two nations, one of which desires to export a portion of its people, or to have its people free to migrate at will. If the value of purity of race shall be firmly established among eugenic principles, it will have strong influence for good concerning the ever-increasing race migrations. The breeding of domestic animals towards some special quality valuable to mankind has nothing to teach concerning the crossing or interbreeding of different human varieties; and all the experiments which have been made, without scientific intention, on the crossing of human varieties,—as, for instance, in the Hawaiian Islands, where the part-Hawaiian population presents the most extraordinary mixture of human stocks in the world,—tend to confirm the principle of race purity; although there are, of course, many instances of fortunate escape by individuals from the deteriorating influence of crossing unlike varieties. The East affords numerous illustrations of the safety of race purity, and of the evil consequences of cross-breeding between dissimilar varieties of the human species. This is not a subject, however, on which exact statistics can be obtained.

The Insecurity of Property Under Despotic Governments

(d) The insecurity of property in the Oriental countries which have been long under despotic government, and the absence of published government budgets covering both receipts and expenses, have widespread consequences unfavorable to public order and international good will throughout the world. Under such governments taxes are not levied and collected under public law by a responsible administration, but are arbitrarily extorted by officials who are expected to fill their own pockets and those of their connections out of the moneys or goods which pass through their hands on the way to the treasury of the despot. A man who makes himself rich, by the intelligent use of his faculties and of such possessions as can be temporarily concealed, is liable to be "squeezed" by the powerful officials of the district in which he lives. When the rich man dies, the property he leaves is liable to be heavily mulcted as it passes to his descendants. Evidently there can be but little accumulation of capital in the hands of a people ruled by such a government. Thus, in China it is well understood that a rich Chinese merchant or manufacturer can be secure in his possessions only on the condition that he live in some foreign concession, where he cannot be "squeezed." If a Chinese trader becomes rich in Singapore, Bangkok, or Penang, or in Java—as he often does—he does not venture to return to his native country with his family, as he would often like to do; because his property, if brought to China, would be subject to the official "squeeze." It follows that the Chinese emigrant who succeeds in the foreign country to which he goes will not bring his wealth home to China, but will die in the foreign land, and there transmit his wealth to his descendants. Just such rich Chinese, resident in foreign parts, have supported the revolution in China with great generosity and public spirit.

Again, the Oriental despot makes no accounting with his subjects concerning his receipts and expenditures. Nobody knows how much his agents succeed in extorting from his subjects, or how he uses, or applies, the money taken from them. Government exists not for the people, but for the despot and his *entourage*. When an Oriental government makes a budget of receipts and expenses, as lately in Siam, and publishes it, or presents it to the national assembly or council, it is taking a long step toward Western constitutional government. The levying of taxes under public law and their collection by public salaried officials who are forbidden to "squeeze" is therefore in Oriental countries a very important step, indeed, an indispensable step, toward the maintenance of public order, the establishment of government for the people, and that security of property which makes possible the accumulation of capital in private hands. Such measures extend the boundaries of civilization, and therefore tend in the long run to promote the peaceful and orderly development of human society.

Liberty of Association and Incorporation

(e) The free governments of the world give to their citizens liberty of association and of incorporation with limited liability for commercial, industrial, educational, religious, and charitable objects. The corporation with limited liability has within seventy years revolutionized the industries of free countries, and greatly increased their productiveness, and has given practice in trusteeship and in the management of the property of many individuals by an elected or deputed agent, to thousands of men who prove themselves capable of discharging such trusts and functions. The corporations with limited liability also offer innumerable opportunities to small investors to place their savings in corporation shares and bonds, which can be readily bought and sold in small amounts, and ordinarily yield a fair return. They are also, as a rule, independent of government aid, and produce by the thousands a kind of manager very different from the government official, and very useful to the community. Some corporations become so large and powerful that they have to be regulated by government; but the great majority of them require no governmental regulation, and serve admirably the consumers of their products, their share-holders, and the public at large. Those which secure a monopoly or a near-monopoly of course have to be regulated by public authority.

In the Orient, incorporation for manufacturing purposes and for planting and mining purposes has been successfully introduced under several of the alien superintending governments, and in Japan the method has already become familiar. A large extension of the method is desirable throughout the Orient, including the new China. Incorporation for educational, charitable, and religious objects is also started in the East, but needs far and wide development. Private persons, through managing corporations for education, charity, and religion, become semi-public administrators, and are themselves being trained in public spirit and sense of trusteeship for others. The method lends great support to free institutions in general, particularly when it becomes strong, as in England and the United States, and competes with government in many modes of promoting the public welfare. It would be difficult to exaggerate the importance of liberty of association and incorporation with limited liability in promoting human welfare and the peace and order which accompany social well-being.

The Administration of Justice

(f) Despotic governments from their very nature are unable to maintain a body of public law, courts to define and enforce that law, and an even-handed administration of justice. The idea of equal laws does not comport with autocratic government; but life and property are never secure in the absence of equal laws and of an administration of justice which commands public confidence; and where life and property are not secure capital may not accumulate, the property of one generation cannot be safely transmitted to another, the family bond is deprived of the support which the sure inheritance of property gives, commerce and manufacturing industries on a large scale cannot be established, and the kind of civilization which has been developed under constitutional government in the nineteenth century is impossible. Hence, misunderstandings, misjudgments, and strifes between East and West. The Western governments thought their "nationals" could not obtain justice in the East through any of the courts of those countries, and therefore insisted on extra-territorial jurisdictions, which were extremely offensive and troublesome to the Oriental governments. Some of these extra-territorial jurisdictions in the East have already been relinquished by the Western powers; and in all probability the time is not far distant when they will all have disappeared. They cannot be given up completely by the Western powers until the administration of justice under the Eastern governments comes to bear a closer resemblance to that which prevails among the Western. Therefore, to advocate the creation of independent legal tribunals and the adoption of a sound administration of justice is to promote peace and good will among men. The success of any government in creating courts which command public confidence will be demonstrated in Oriental countries by an increase of litigation; for people keep out of courts where judgments are bought and sold, but resort to the independent and upright judge. The best thing the British government has done for its Indian and Egyptian subjects is the establishment of numerous courts of all grades which command the confidence of the Indian and Egyptian business public. It should be observed, however, that in countries where the Mohammedan element in the population is large, there is serious difficulty in introducing such courts and legal practices as the Christian peoples, and particularly those of Teutonic origin, long since adopted; because the ideas of justice and mercy, and of punishment and forgiveness which Moslems derive from the Koran are very different from those which the Christian nations entertain, and have confidently applied in practice for centuries without apparently noticing that their penological methods habitually fail to prevent crime—though they restrict it—to reform criminals, or to improve public morals. In regard to the treatment of criminals, and of young persons who exhibit criminal propensities, civilized society under any or all of the great religions has beneficent changes in store for a future not remote.

The Regulation of the Vices

(g) Throughout the Far East the regulation of the opium traffic, of the sale of alcoholic beverages, of gambling houses, and of prostitution, is very imperfect, and in many of the seaports has hardly been attempted. Sometimes regulation has been attempted for natives, and sometimes for foreigners, but seldom for both. It is the Orientals that most need to be defended from the opium habit and from gambling, the Occidentals from the alcoholic habit, and both from prostitution. The disease and misery which result from these vices in the Far East are indescribable, particularly in the seaports and other large cities. All the Western governments need to be urged to grapple with the terrible evils these vices engender, to put restraints on the viciously inclined, and to defend the innocent from contagions due to vice. At present, in many parts of the East the opium trade, the public bar, the gambling house, and the brothel are regarded as sources of revenue, so that they are licensed and somewhat restricted, but not suppressed. The licenses under some governments are sold to the highest bidder; so that the government's chief concern thereafter is to prevent illegitimate interference with the business of the purchaser of the license. In some of the British colonies the sale of such licenses yields a not unimportant part of the colonial revenue.

Comparative Legislation in Western Dependencies in the Far East

In respect to the above seven well-recognized means (a-g) of promoting well-being and happiness among any people that has lived long under despotic government, there are considerable differences of legislation and practice in the dependencies of Great Britain, France, and The Netherlands, and even among the different British dependencies in the Far East, namely, India, Ceylon, Burma, Straits Settlements, and the Federated Malay States. Inasmuch as the legislation and practice of any one of these European governments, or of any one dependency of a single government, are liable to be much influenced by successful action taken in some other government or dependency in regard to education, preventive medicine, labor, taxation, incorporation, public justice, and the limitation of vices, it is desirable that fresh, comparative statements of actual legislation and practice on the matters above mentioned in all the superintended countries should be prepared at short intervals by impartial agents, and distributed freely to government officials throughout the East, and to publicists and private societies and agencies interested in those subjects, whether in the Orient or the Occident.

I suggest, therefore, that the Carnegie Endowment for International Peace employ at once a competent scholar to prepare such a comparative statement of existing laws and practice in the European dependencies in the East. The details of this suggestion will be communicated to the Trustees in a separate statement.

The Causes of War Have Changed

Advocacy of these slow-acting means of preventing wars in the East implies that within the superintended areas the probable causes of international war have changed within fifty years. Dynastic and religious wars, and wars in support of despotic government are no longer probable; and racial antipathies are held in check by the superintending European powers in all the countries to which that superintendence extends. Thus, the Pax Britannica has practically put an end to the racial and religious warfare which from time to time desolated the Asiatic countries over which British influence now extends. Small outbreaks of racial antipathy or religious fanaticism occur locally; but these are insignificant exceptions to the prevailing tranquillity. The fighting Great Britain has done to establish and maintain this quieting influence has been fighting on a small scale compared with that which went on among European nations during the nineteenth century, or among Oriental peoples in many earlier centuries, and the Pax Britannica has therefore been a great contribution to the peace of the world.

It is not only in the East that the probable causes of international war have lately changed. All over the world, it is reasonable to suppose that wars for dynastic motives will occur no more, and that religious motives for warfare will hereafter be incidental or secondary instead of primary. It is also reasonable to believe that wars in support of absolute monarchs and despotic government will henceforth be unknown, so general is the world-wide movement towards constitutional government and free institutions—a movement from fifty to three hundred and fifty years old among the different nations of the West, but comparatively recent in the East.

The Future Causes of War

What, then, will be the probable causes of international war in the future?

The causes of war in the future are likely to be national distrusts, dislikes, and apprehensions, which have been nursed in ignorance, and fed on rumors, suspicions, and conjectures propagated by unscrupulous newsmongers, until suddenly developed by some untoward event into active hatred, or widespread alarm which easily passes into panic. While the Eastern peoples—Far and Near—will have some causes of their own for war, because in some instances neither their geographical limits nor their governmental institutions are as yet settled, among the Western peoples the most probable future causes of war, in addition to national antipathies, will be clashing commercial or industrial interests, contests for new markets and fresh opportunities for profitable investments of capital, and possibly, extensive migrations of laborers. All modern governments, in which life, liberty, and property are secured by public law, desire to extend the commerce and trade of their people, to develop their home industries by procuring markets for their products in foreign lands, to obtain in comparatively unoccupied or undeveloped parts of the earth opportunities for the profitable employment of their accumulated capital, and to gain room for a possible surplus of population in the future. Eastern and Western peoples alike feel the desire for a large, strong governmental unit, too formidable to be attacked from without, too cohesive to be disintegrated from within. Both East and West exhibit the modern irrepressible objection to alien rule, especially when such rule, like that of the Manchus or the Turks, produces poverty and desolation, denies liberty, and prevents progress.

Several Western nations, which have the saving, or accumulating, habit, are eager to make loans to remote and comparatively poor nations which are in great need of money to pay for costly public works of transportation, conservancy, public health, and public security. In making such loans the bankers of each Western nation expect the support and protection of their own government. As security for such loans the borrowing government, national, provincial, or municipal, pledges some of its resources; and if the expected interest or dividend is not paid, the lender forecloses. Hence serious international complications. In this lending business the Western powers come into competition with each other, and stimulated by mutual jealousies, engage in aggressive operations against the Oriental peoples, who have been as a rule helpless in their hands, until Japan adopted and improved on the Western military organization and methods of fighting, and succeeded for a short time in borrowing the money needed to pay the heavy costs of modern warfare.

The penetration of Oriental territories by traders and missionaries has given occasion for many attacks by Western powers on Oriental governments and peoples, on the theory that the citizen or subject of a Western government is to be protected by his own government, wherever he may wander or settle in Oriental communities. If any such adventurous citizen is harmed, there follows a "punitive expedition" with wholesale destruction of innocent property and life, and often an extension of the "sphere of influence" of the punisher. This protection of missionaries, traders, and travellers has often been the cause, or in many cases the excuse, for attacks by Western powers on Oriental communities, for the seizure of valuable ports and of territory adjacent thereto and for the enforced payment of exaggerated indemnities which heavily burden later generations. Hence long-continued international dislikes and distrusts.

A people which has for centuries been under despotic rule will not have accumulated any considerable masses of capital, because private property will not have been safe from arbitrary seizure, and cannot have been transmitted safely from generation to generation. Throughout the East, therefore, the capital which is seeking investment in mines, plantations, factories, transportation companies, and so forth, is Western capital, and is likely to be for at least another generation, or until Japan and China can reap the full benefit of the security of capital under constitutional government. The Orient as a whole, and China in particular, will need for many years the continuous investment of Western capital in great public works, such as roads, railroads, defenses against flood, drought, and pestilences, schools, universities, and a civil service which lives on salaries, and collects and expends honestly a stable public revenue. As soon as the Republic of China can provide itself with a stable public revenue, it will come into the markets of the world for an indefinite series of large loans; and all the Western peoples will be eager to share in the lending. Japan, too, will need for many years large amounts of capital for the furtherance of its governmental and industrial changes.

Through all the Oriental countries the mass of the people maintain a lower standard of living than that of any civilized Western people, whether European or American. This is partly a matter of climate and of density of population; but it is also a matter of tradition and custom. When the standard of living is close to the limits essential to the maintenance of health and bodily vigor, natural catastrophes like droughts, floods, earthquakes, and pestilences cause recurrent periods of immense human misery, from which recovery is slow. The misery of these masses in turn seriously depresses the courage or enterprise of the suffering nation, and commerce, trade, and manufacturing industries throughout the world, particularly in those Oriental countries where modern means of transportation and communication have not been adequately developed. Hence, frequent interruptions of trade, and disorders both interior and exterior; and hence, also, troublesome migrations. The chronic poverty of multitudinous Oriental peoples hinders the desired development of Western industries and commerce; because the poverty-stricken millions cannot afford to buy the Western goods. To prevent such widespread miseries and such chronic poverty would be to remove the cause of many of the violences which break out from time to time in Oriental communities, and provoke or promote the intrusion of the stronger Western powers. Successful prevention would imply sound legislation, efficient local administration, and the liberal expenditure of money. Advocacy of such measures and help in executing them would promote peace and good will. Here is a great field for Western benevolence, skilfully applying private endowments to public uses.

Some of the worst dissensions between Eastern and Western peoples have been caused in recent years by the dense ignorance and gross superstitions of Oriental populations. A good example of the contentions due to these causes is the Boxer insurrection in China, against which several Western powers took arms—when their Legations were attacked—with success so far as subduing the insurrection and procuring huge indemnities from China went, but with deplorable effects on the disposition of the Chinese people toward Japan and all the Western powers that sent troops to Peking, with the single exception of the United States. The only real cure for ignorance and superstition is universal education, and that cure will take time.

The Fear of Invasion

Although the causes of war tend to become commercial and industrial, two other world-wide causes of war remain which are liable to take effect at any time in both the East and the West. The first is the fear of sudden invasion by an overwhelming force. This fear is as keenly felt in China and Japan as it is in Germany, France, and England; and there are no better defenses against it in the East than in the West. The neutralization of territory which protects some of the small European nations, like Switzerland and Belgium, rests rather upon the mutual jealousy of the greater powers than on any established practice among the European peoples, or any trustworthy sense of expediency and justice. The nearest approach in the East to the practice of neutralizing territory is the respect paid by the larger European powers to the Eastern possessions of smaller powers. Thus, England and France are respecting the Oriental possessions of The Netherlands and of Portugal; and all nations are now respecting the outlying possessions of Japan. Whether the Eastern possessions of Western powers will in the future be transferred from one nation to another as a consequence of the issue of European conflicts—as they have been in the past—is a problem for the future. The only hope in the East, as in the West, for relief from this terrible apprehension of invasion lies in the progress of international law, and in the spreading opinion among publicists that there are better ways than war to settle international questions about territory, commercial intercourse, and sovereignty. This is a region in which all three divisions of the activities of the Carnegie Endowment for International Peace are nearly concerned—Intercourse and Education, Economics, and International Law.

The Exemption of Private Property From Capture at Sea

The other apprehension which may at any time become the cause of war is the fear lest the supplies of food and raw material which come to a country over seas should be cut off. Such insular countries as Great Britain and Japan are peculiarly subject to this apprehension; for either of them would be seriously distressed by even a short interruption of its supplies of food and raw material. Both these nations are therefore obliged to maintain navies more powerful than any likely to be brought against them. Hence the immense burdens of competitive naval armaments. A remedy for this apprehension is, however, in sight. The doctrine that private property should be exempt from capture at sea, as it is already exempted from seizure without compensation on land, will, when adopted by a few nations which maintain strong navies, relieve the nations adopting it from the dread lest their food supplies and the supply of raw materials for their manufacturing industries should be cut off, and the export of their manufactured goods be made impossible or unsafe. To secure relief from this recurrent apprehension which prompts such exorbitant expenditure on navies, it would not be necessary that all the nations of the world should adopt the doctrine of the exemption of private property at sea from capture. Five or six of the stronger nations, adopting it and enforcing it against all comers, could immediately secure relief for themselves, and for any other nations that chose to join them in the adoption of the policy. The United States has advocated this doctrine for many years; but an effective adoption of it has been prevented by the reluctance of Great Britain to abandon the practice of seizing upon the ocean private property belonging to the subjects of her enemy. There are some signs that Great Britain is approaching the conclusion that she has more to gain than to lose by the adoption of the policy of exemption.

The Occidental Desire for Ports, Concessions, and Spheres of Influence in the East

A common reason for the aggressions of Western powers in Eastern countries has been their desire to possess or control ports in the East through which

Western trade with the teeming Oriental populations could be safely conducted. Great Britain, France, Germany, and The Netherlands all possess some ports, and in China the first three powers exercise a strong control over other ports by means of treaties and leases forced upon China. Russia's keen desire for better ports in Eastern waters than she now possesses has been a leading motive in her Eastern policy for many years. The statesmen of Japan felt that it was absolutely necessary for her to possess the ports of the Korean peninsula. When once a nation gets possession of ports which originally and properly made part of another nation's territory, the possessing nation feels that it must defend them against all comers; hence incessant preparations for war and ever-increasing armaments. The peace of the world would be promoted if no nation, Occidental or Oriental, possessed or controlled a port on another nation's territory.

The peace of the world is also threatened by the constant efforts of most of the trading nations to enlarge their territories, or "spheres of influence" in remote parts of the world, whether sparsely or densely populated. It seems to make little difference whether these enlargements are likely to be profitable or not; they will be acquired at a venture.

In Europe and America, the creation of new and large units of government went on actively during the last half of the nineteenth century, and is still in progress by natural growth and new affiliations. Among political theorists doubts begin to be expressed about the expediency of these very large units of national territory and government. Evidence has been produced that the smaller nations in Europe are more prosperous than the larger; perhaps because they waste less on armies, navies, and armaments. There are those who think that China would be better off if Thibet, Mongolia, and Manchuria should be absorbed respectively by Great Britain, Russia, and Japan, leaving the eighteen provinces of China proper as a compact and manageable whole. These objections to exaggerated size still remain in the region of speculation and not of practice; and the desire of trading nations for more and always more territory remains a threatening source of international contests.

Alien Government

Recent events, however, in both the Near and the Far East indicate clearly that the government of large populations by an alien race is getting increasingly difficult, and may in time become impossible. The unrest in India, the abdication of the Manchus in China, and the Balkan war all illustrate the fact that the government of large populations by an alien authority is likely to be more and more resented and ultimately resisted; and that no amount of good will and good works by an alien government will be able to overcome the opposition of native races to such a government, just because it *is* alien. Because of the strength and vitality of this racial sentiment against alien government, it is likely that the task of governing and supervising large native populations from a distance by rulers, judges, and administrators of a very different race will prove to be increasingly troublesome and costly; so that freedom of commerce and trade will come to be sought by other means.

On March 22, 1912, I arrived at Hongkong, and entered at once upon study of the effects of the revolution in China, and of public opinion in regard to it among both Chinese and foreign residents. Dr. Sun Yat Sen had resigned his temporary presidency, and Yuan Shih Kai had been chosen Provisional President, and was established at Peking, where a cabinet for the President was being slowly assembled.

The Revolution in China

I learnt at once that the new government was in great straits for money, had been unable to pay and disband the superfluous revolutionary levies, and had also been unable to prevent local disorders, which were chargeable in most instances to unpaid and insubordinate revolutionary soldiers. After a few days at Hongkong I visited Canton, where the provisional government of Kwangtung Province was seated, and there had my first interview with Chinese republican officials. I talked with the temporary Governor-General, who was a general in the revolutionary army, and with several members of his cabinet, and learnt that very little progress had been made towards settling such fundamental constitutional questions as the qualifications for the suffrage and the division of powers between the central government and the provincial governments. A strong educational qualification for the suffrage seemed to be practically determined on; but the question of a property qualification was open. The Governor-General favored an adequate educational qualification but no property qualification. In reply to a question from me, he said, as a result of his recent experience in the field, that the Chinese coolie made a good soldier, if he knew what he was fighting about, and the object of the fighting had an interest for him. Under those conditions the coolie had in him the making of a brave, obedient soldier, capable of great exertions, ready to endure hardships and wounds, and indifferent to death. In conversation with several of his cabinet officers, I heard without surprise that southern China was very different from northern China, had different political aspirations, had been long prepared for the revolution, and felt serious doubts about the republicanism of the new President. It was admitted that the Kwangtung Province was in a disorderly state, that there had been many piracies and robberies, and that the Provincial Government was trying to maintain order under great difficulties. For instance, many of the revolutionary troops were not fully uniformed; so that the populace had difficulty in distinguishing between legitimate armed bands and illegitimate. The state of the public mind was, however, much calmer than it had been three months earlier, the characteristic industries of Canton and the vicinity were returning to their normal state, the provincial revenues were being collected in good measure, and traffic was resuming its customary proportions.

Some striking changes in the customs of the people were visible at once. Queues, or pigtails, on men had disappeared in Kwangtung Province. European clothing had been adopted by a large proportion of the educated class, and all ceremonies had been abandoned in intercourse with officials. I met the officials, to whom I was presented, with no more ceremony than would be observed in a Washington Department, or a city bank, or the treasurer's office of a large factory in the United States. At a luncheon with eight or ten of the Provisional Cabinet officers, I learnt from the personal testimony of several of the gentlemen present that the revolution had been long prepared, although it broke out of a sudden at Hankow and Wuchang earlier than the revolutionary leaders had expected or desired. One gentleman, who had been educated in an American college, testified that he had personally worked in the revolutionary cause for more than twenty five years, at the risk of his life and career, and had had many hairbreadth escapes. The revolution had been prepared through secret societies which extended all over China, but were stronger in south and middle China than in north China. For pecuniary support these societies were much indebted to rich Chinese, who had made their money in some of the British or Dutch possessions in the East, and were strongly interested in promoting the cause of constitutional government in China, since they could not return with their wealth to their native land until a modern government had been established there.

The foreign residents in Hongkong and Canton felt small confidence in the new government; but admitted that trade was returning to its former volume, and that the country in general was more orderly than it was three months before. Nevertheless, the sand-bag barricades were still standing in some of the streets of the foreign concession at Canton; and the barbed wire entanglements along the river bank had not been wholly removed; and when I paid my visit to the Governor-General, an armed guard accompanied the party, although it could not have been effective in the narrow streets.

One of the promptest effects of the revolution was brought to my attention in Hongkong by a Chinese merchant who was personally supporting a small newspaper chiefly devoted to furthering the cause of the revolution. It appeared that a large number of newspapers printed in Chinese had suddenly come into existence to enjoy the unwonted freedom of public discussion. The publication of the great majority of these newspapers was unremunerative; but they were kept in circulation by the public spirit of their proprietors. Their language was often violent; but with only a few exceptions they had not been interfered with by the new government, either national or provincial.

It was an indication of the unsettled state of the province that the European managers of the new railroad from Canton to Kowloon, opposite Hongkong, did not venture to run any trains by night, because of the great risk of interference with the trains by bands bent on pillage. It was interesting to meet in the general manager's car on that railroad a grandson of Garibaldi, who was one of the division superintendents.

The Physical and Moral Qualities of the Chinese

One cannot be even a few days in contact with a crowded Chinese population without being deeply impressed with the laboriousness, industry, patience, and cheerfulness of the people as a whole. It was my first sight of a country in which the principal source of mechanical power was human muscle. I had never before seen a city's traffic for both passengers and freight conducted chiefly by men, pulling or pushing small carts on one wheel or more, and carrying enormous burdens on their backs. I had never before seen women managing large rowboats without any assistance from men, and often carrying babies on their backs while rowing. I had never before seen a laborer's life so strenuous during long hours, and so absolutely devoid of comfort during eating and sleeping, as one sees it in all Chinese cities. The tough physical and moral qualities of the Chinese obtrude themselves on the stranger's notice from the first moment of his arrival in the country, and show him why the hundreds of millions of Chinese have arrived at our day through every possible hardship and suffering, through unknown centuries of despotic government, through pestilences, droughts, famines, and floods, and are here in unnumbered millions to take part in a very extraordinary governmental transformation.

The Chinese Have No Knowledge of Western Medicine

Not only have the people of China been subject to terrible occasional pestilences, against which they have had no defense, but they have also been subject to the ravages of the ordinary contagious diseases known in Europe and America, and to other tropical or semi-tropical diseases which rarely occur in the more temperate regions of Western civilization. They have had no knowledge of the practice of scientific medicine, and no knowledge of surgery in the modern sense. The Chinese physician uses various drugs and medicaments compounded of strange materials, employs charms and incantations, and claims occult powers, and he is always willing to puncture any gathering on the human body which seems capable of yielding a liquid to the hollow needle; but of scientific diagnosis, major surgery, anesthesia, and asepsis he knows nothing. He is not acquainted with any of the optical, acoustical, and electrical apparatus which the Western physician uses; and he possesses none of the modern chemical and bacteriological means of diagnosis. Hence the treatment of disease in the mass of the Chinese population is ignorant, superstitious, and almost completely ineffectual. The tea-drinking habit of the people has secured them in good measure from the dangers of drinking infected water; and the fact that nearly every mother nurses her baby has protected infants from the dangers which attend the Western use of cow's milk for babies. Tuberculosis is terribly destructive throughout China; and the family habit of sleeping all together in a single small room, with every aperture tightly closed to keep out imps and demons, spreads the disease.

The Missionary Medical Services

Here, then, is a great gift that the West can make to China,—scientific medicine and surgery. Of late years the various missionary boards domiciled in Western countries have turned their attention to medical missionary work in China, and have begun to commend Christianity to the Chinese through the beneficent ministries of hospitals and infirmaries. Unfortunately, the missionary boards at home have not appreciated in general the cost of such establishments, or the amount of knowledge and skill which an isolated medical practitioner in China needs to have at his fingers' ends. Accordingly, the missionary medical services have not yielded the fruits which might have been expected of them. During my stay in China I paid special attention to the missionary hospitals and infirmaries; but never saw one which did not urgently need more physicians and surgeons, more nurses, and more expenditure for service and supplies. The devotion of the missionaries in this field was admirable; but their resources were always inadequate, and they were often unable to meet fully urgent demands on their skill and benevolence. Under such conditions both men and women are overworked, deteriorate in their own technique, and become callous to the disastrous conditions under which they are compelled to treat their patients. Any Western organization which desires to promote friendly intercourse with an Oriental people can do nothing better than contribute to the introduction of Western medicine, surgery, and sanitation into China. The field for such beneficent work is immense, the obstacles to be overcome are serious but not insuperable, and the reward in the future comparative well-being of the Chinese is sure. The Chinese people are too intelligent not to trace practical beneficence to its spiritual sources, and to draw all the just inferences.

From British Hongkong I went to Shanghai, where I had interviews with Dr. Sun Yat Sen and the Premier, Tong Shao Yi, who chanced to be staying for a few days in that city. These gentlemen both talked hopefully of the progress made in organizing the new government and quieting the country, but sadly about the very scanty revenues of the new Republic and the pressure of the foreign powers on the provisional central government at Peking. From both of these officials I received the impression that the revolution was the work of young men, educated abroad after having received at home the traditional training in the Chinese classics. The students who had returned home within ten years from Europe, America, and Japan formed an important part of the intellectual and physical force which had inaugurated the revolution, and brought it thus far on its way. These returned students have brought back to China the fundamental idea of government for the people, and the conception in regard to all modern governments that they exist to promote the general welfare of the entire people, and are to be judged solely by the measure of their success in that work.

The Manchus Gone Forever

At Shanghai I began to encounter resident foreigners who for some months after the outbreak of the revolution had believed it would be possible to set up what they called a constitutional government in China, with a Manchu monarch at the head of it; but most of these persons had already changed their minds, and come to the belief that the Manchu Empire had gone forever. This was the belief of all the Chinese gentlemen with whom I conversed. They unanimously dismissed the idea of a constitutional monarchy with a Manchu monarch. They alleged first, that it was impossible to find such a monarch; secondly, that it would be impossible to secure Chinese capable of filling the cabinet offices and conducting an effective administration in the face of an inexperienced Chinese parliament; and thirdly, that under Chinese conditions it was really much easier to set up a dictatorship with republican forms than a constitutional monarchy with its government by parties, its elaborate constitutional checks and balances, and its liability to sudden and frequent changes of administration. I heard often from American and British residents that it was absurd to suppose that the masses of the Chinese population, ignorant, superstitious, and accustomed to despotic government, could carry on safely any sort of a republic; but the Chinese answer to this statement was always ready: "We are not proposing to set up a government based on universal suffrage, but on a suffrage closely limited by an educational test." For such a republic the Chinese are not wholly unprepared. There has always been in their manners and customs a large element of democracy; the people have been accustomed in many parts of China to a good degree of local self-government; Chinese official life was open to all sorts of people on a high educational test; and finally, the ordinary Chinese are enduring, patient, industrious, honest, and chiefly concerned, each man and each family, with their own affairs.

The Imperial Maritime Customs Service

At Shanghai I had the best possible opportunities to appreciate the great service which Sir Robert Hart rendered to China in organizing and carrying on for more than a generation the Imperial Maritime Customs Service. This great Service not only collected the customs, and applied the receipts to the payment of the interest on and the reduction of Chinese public loans, but also carried on the lighthouse and day-mark service for the coasts and rivers of

China, and planned and executed many important conservancy undertakings in and near the treaty ports.

At the same time, I came to understand why Chinese administrators are resentful toward the Customs Service, and use the Service as an illustration of the inexpediency of committing Chinese affairs to foreign executive officers, no matter how honest and competent they may be. The Republican officials today point out that the Imperial Customs Service in more than forty years has not trained a single competent Chinese official for service in any high office under the present government. They point out that Sir Robert Hart never gave a Chinese any but a very subordinate position in his great Service, all the high and medium posts being filled with foreigners. They remember, too, that the receipts from customs have been, and must be, appropriated under existing treaties to pay the interest on loans which China was forced to make in order to pay to Western powers war expenses and indemnities.

The Republican officials had another reason for hesitating to employ foreign advisers in the many departments of the government where their services would be convenient, if not indispensable. They cited numerous instances in which the Chinese government has selected and employed foreigners who have turned out to be unworthy and unsuccessful; and they averred that Chinese administrators are seldom competent to select the right kind of foreign advisers, being often unable to discriminate between the good and the bad, either on personal interviews or by inquiry into the careers of the candidates. They allege an inability to understand Westerners analogous to the supposed incapacity of Westerners to comprehend Chinese manners, ethics, and modes of reasoning. They object also to accepting foreign advisers on the nomination of foreign governments, because of the jealousies and prepossessions which such nominees are wont to represent.

The Manchu Empire Had No Proper Revenues

It was at Shanghai that I first got a clear impression of the extremely narrow resources of the new government. The salt-tax seemed to be the only sure reliance for a national revenue; and in regard to that tax it was admitted that the manufacture of salt by the government was badly conducted, that the product was dirty and otherwise impure, and that it would take some time to reform the manufacture under expert advice to be procured from Italy or Austria. The Manchus left to the Republic no government organization in the modern sense, and no national resources to speak of. They turned over to the Republic no trustworthy army, no efficient navy, no roads, no schools, no national system of taxation, no national police, no courts or body of laws in the Western sense, no public health service, and no control of mines or railroads. It did bequeath to the Republic numerous embarrassing concessions made to foreign governments and foreign corporations, and many crippling treaties whereby proper national resources are pawned or their development is hindered. In short, the Empire fulfilled none of the purposes of a modern government for the people, and had nothing to turn over to the Republic.

There has never been a census of the Chinese people, and there exists no survey of the land to serve as a basis for a system of taxation. Several years before the abdication of the Manchus, Sir Robert Hart recommended a land tax which would have yielded an adequate revenue for the national as distinguished from the provincial governments; and he maintained that the revenue could be collected within three years by organizing gradually, in one province after another, a just and competent collecting agency. To this admirable and attractive proposal the Manchu government never paid any attention, being satisfied with the tribute they received at Peking from the provinces of the Empire for the support of the Imperial household and the Manchu clan.

The present Republican government is afraid to adopt this land tax, first, lest it should prove obnoxious to the people at the starting of the new government, and secondly, because they think it might take ten years, instead of three, to make the necessary survey and organize the collecting agency. Never was a more complete demonstration given by a retiring government that it had been nothing but a sham, lacking both the wish and the purpose to serve the people governed. If the Republic shall accomplish nothing else than to deliver the Chinese from their Manchu rulers, it will have deserved the gratitude of the Chinese people and the admiration of mankind.

Two Useful Institutions at Shanghai

Two institutions established at Shanghai promote mutual good will and good understanding between Chinese and foreigners,—the International Institute of China, which labors to remove the barriers now separating the Chinese from foreigners and to cultivate friendly intercourse through social meetings, publications, lectures, classroom instruction, and discussion of public affairs with leading Chinese, and the Christian Literature Society for China, which for many years has been issuing at low prices books, tracts, and manuals in Chinese, and also maps, diagrams, and pictures. The Christian Literature Society's list of publications includes many scientific and economic books and pamphlets, as well as theological, historical, and religious literature. The two societies are alike in respect to their fundamental aim, which is to increase mutual knowledge between the educated Chinese on the one hand and the resident Occidentals on the other, and to make known Occidental ideals and modes of thought to educated Chinese.

The founders and directors of these two societies, Rev. Gilbert Reid for the International Institute of China, and Rev. Timothy Richard for the Christian Literature Society for China, were both originally missionaries. Both have worked long in China, and are thoroughly acquainted with the Chinese character and with the needs of Chinese society. Both have had strong influence among educated Chinese, both Christian and non-Christian. Their labors have done something to establish sympathetic relations between educated foreigners resident in China and the whole class of Chinese readers and thinkers. Their labors have transcended the usual bounds of missionary effort, and have helped to mitigate the extraordinary ignorance of the Chinese people in which commercial foreigners who spend many years in China are apt to remain. (See Appendix I.)

Education Among the Chinese

From Shanghai I went to Tientsin, reaching that treaty port on April 13, and remaining there till June 8, making, however, three excursions, two to Peking (one of which included a journey to the great wall and the Ming Tombs), and one to Paoting-fu. My absences from Tientsin covered two and a half weeks, so that I passed five and a half weeks in Tientsin. This city is a place of considerable commercial importance, but it is also the best place in China in which to study Chinese educational conditions and institutions. The Chinese people as a whole have had for many centuries a high appreciation of the value of education; and prolonged intellectual training has been the only avenue to official station. The nature, or quality of education in China has remained unchanged for more than two thousand years; it has always been an education exclusively literary, with some small additions of a historical and metaphysical nature. In the elementary schools of China young children began to commit to memory phrases and sentences from the writing of Confucius and his commentators, years before they could possibly understand the meaning of those phrases; and children and youths did little else at later stages of their training, the staple of instruction remaining the same through the entire period of systematic education. The learning to recognize and write correctly thousands of Chinese characters called for another great feat of memory. The ultimate object in view was the passing of the State examinations which admitted the student to the official class; and the passing of these examinations was chiefly a feat of memory. A Chinese scholar twenty five years of age had probably received no manual training, and had learnt the use of no tools except his writing implements, had acquired no knowledge whatever of the inductive method, and had never heard of any of the modern Western sciences. Moreover, he had been trained to no out-of-door sports, and had no habit of taking bodily exercise. Although the elementary schools in China were accessible to a large proportion of the children on small payments by their parents, most of the children soon showed themselves incapable of profiting by memory training of the sort the schools invariably provided; so that the educated class never constituted more than a very small proportion of the entire nation.

The grave consequences of this method of education and of the resulting qualities of the educated class are strongly illustrated in the present political situation of the country. The popular respect for education makes a high educational qualification for the suffrage seem entirely natural and proper; and explains the fact that a few thousand young, educated Chinese were able to enlist hundreds of thousands of illiterate but patriotic soldiers in the cause of the revolution. Although many of the active promoters of the revolution had been educated in America, Europe, and Japan, and had there acquired the modern idea of government for the people, and had learnt the elements of some of the applied sciences, it was found very difficult to fill the upper positions in the new government with Chinese competent to discharge effectively the modern functions of government administrators, almost all of which today require some familiarity with the applications of the chemical, physical, and biological sciences. The Provisional Republic needed men physically able to endure arduous labors under conditions full of danger and anxiety. The physical and mental incapacity for government work of an educated class which has been brought up without athletic sports and out-of-door exercise, without experience in army or navy service, and without knowledge of the applied sciences, is painfully visible in the China of today. The Chinese student and scholar did nothing in the way of physical labor, for manual labor was beneath his dignity. Physical vigor and endurance were not to be expected of him. The Republic desires to break with all these educational and social traditions; but it must have time to effect so great a change.

The Transformation of Chinese Education

In their last years the Manchus had resolved to set up in China several institutions of learning, which should give a training in the Western sciences while maintaining a considerable portion of the Chinese literary training. They established, for example, the Pei Yang University at Tientsin, and an Army Medical School in the same city; but these new institutions had been only a few years in operation when the revolution broke out. The new institutions illustrated the ill effects of mutual jealousies among the Western Powers, which for two generations had been afflicting China. It was of course desirable that one European language should be the vehicle of all the sciences in the new institutions; and obviously English was far the best language for that purpose; but to satisfy Germany and France it was necessary to have the German and French languages placed on an equality with the English in the programs, a measure which added considerably to the cost of maintaining the colleges and universities without any corresponding advantage to the students.

The expiring Empire accepted the unwelcome necessity of employing large numbers of foreigners to teach in its new educational institutions; but retained in the programs of study so large a proportion of the students' time for the study of the Chinese classics that too small a proportion was allotted to the Western sciences, to modern economics, and to Western law. The Republic has already formed a project for reducing largely the time to be allotted to the old *memoriter* study of the Chinese classics, thus making room for more liberal use of Western subjects and the inductive method. Many of the young republicans had attended the colleges and universities of Japan, and had there seen the extraordinary transformation in elementary, secondary, and professional education which the Japanese had brought about within a single generation. All these men are ambitious to see a similar change wrought in China at the earliest day possible; but they are well aware that to bring about this change the whole system of Chinese education must be reconstructed from bottom to top.

The difficulties of introducing an adequate teaching of modern surgery into China were illustrated in the failure of the Army Medical School at Tientsin to produce surgeons who could be of use in time of war. Because of the veneration of ancestors and of the burial practices which that veneration has produced, the schools of Western medicine heretofore established in China, including the Government school in Tientsin, have been unable to provide their pupils with opportunities for dissection and the proper study of operative surgery, and at this moment in China the only medical school which can teach these subjects adequately to Chinese students is the Harvard Medical School of China at Shanghai. This new school is established on a British concession in a city having a considerable foreign population in addition to a large Chinese population, and controlled in respect to sanitation by a British health officer. In March, 1912, a good deal of fighting occurred in the vicinity of Tientsin and Peking, in which regiments were concerned which had been supplied with surgeons from the Army Medical School at Tientsin; but in the field these surgeons turned out to be wholly useless. They could not operate successfully on the wounded, and were afraid to try. Their School had provided them with theoretical instruction, but had given them no adequate opportunity to acquire the necessary skill of eye and hand. Now the biological sciences and the skills of the physician and surgeon are the most needed in China of all the Occidental sciences and skills; for China is at present without defense against the pestilences, the ordinary contagious diseases, and the traumatic accidents. Yet physicians, surgeons, and public health officers cannot be adequately trained in China, until the republican government has succeeded in reconciling the population to the dissection of the human body—a very serious undertaking. Meantime, China will continue to exhibit a condition of medical practice which curiously resembles that of Europe during the Middle Ages, before the advent in Europe of the inductive method of arriving at truth.

Influence of Mission Schools and Colleges on Chinese Education

The mission schools and colleges which have been set up in China by American and European boards have exerted a good influence on Chinese education through the introduction of some elementary training in the sciences, and also through the introduction of athletic sports. The Young Men's Christian Associations have been useful in the same directions, but particularly in the introduction of sports. It was not to be expected, however, that the mission schools should diminish very much the proportion of time devoted by Chinese boys and youths to literary and memory studies, because the teaching of a Western language was inevitably an important part of the total teaching of mission schools, and also because Western schools and colleges themselves are still giving altogether too small an amount of attention to the training of the senses, to the experimental sciences, and to the inductive philosophy. The mission schools and colleges are of course obliged to take no inconsiderable portion of the time of their pupils for Bible lessons, and lessons on Christian history and biography, all of which are plain memory work analogous to the Chinese memorizing of the Confucian classics.

Changes in Chinese Education Essential to National Unity

Upon profound changes in the system of Chinese education the unification of the Republic obviously depends. A common speech—Mandarin—is urgently needed to displace the numerous local dialects, a training of the rising generation in elementary science, in exact observation and faithful record is required, and thereafter a thorough mastery by a select few of the applied sciences which are indispensable in the administration of a modern government. These changes cannot be wrought without extensive modification of the religious traditions and beliefs of the common people, although there is no unity of religious belief in China, but on the contrary an ingrained diversity. To accomplish such a prodigious task as this the new government must be allowed at least one generation, after it has secured a stable national revenue.

Travelling Fellowships for Chinese Graduates

In what way can the Carnegie Endowment wisely contribute to the transformation of Chinese education? First, by providing travelling fellowships for graduates of Chinese institutions, each available for professional study anywhere in the United States for a period not exceeding four years, the incumbents to be selected by the Chinese government's Department of Education, and the income of each fellowship to be one thousand dollars ($1,000) a year and the cost of one journey from China to the United States and return. If the number of these fellowships should be twenty, at least five young Chinese would return to their country each year, well trained in those Occidental knowledges and skills which are most needed in the China of today. If the number were forty, at least ten young men would return annually. The Chinese students who have returned during the past thirty years from the Occident and from Japan have already demonstrated, under the most unfavorable conditions, that they are capable of exerting a strong beneficent influence on their countrymen. Under the Republic, if it procure a stable and adequate revenue, the conditions for returning students will be much more favorable; so that no one can now imagine—much less portray—the good results of supplying to China a steady stream of from five to ten young men, competent to bring to bear on Chinese affairs the best principles and methods of both Oriental and Occidental civilization.

Another effective method of aiding the development of Chinese education in an important field would be to build and carry on at Tientsin a hospital for Chinese patients, equipped and maintained in the best way, and officered by American physicians and surgeons aided by a competent corps of nurses and orderlies. This work would have three objects in view,—first, to show the Chinese how to carry on an active hospital in the best Occidental manner; secondly, to show them the beneficial results which may be expected from such a hospital in the relief of suffering, the saving of life, and the prevention of disease; and thirdly, to illustrate in thousands of individual cases the practical beneficence of Occidental medicine and surgery. The teaching of such a hospital in China would not be given by talking about love and beneficence, but by actually doing good; not by memorizing maxims, proverbs, and ethical principles, but by doing with skilful eyes, ears, and hands works of mercy, hope, and prevention. With such a hospital should be connected a training school for nurses; so that through its agency family, district, and municipal nursing would be gradually introduced into China. It has been abundantly proved in Western communities that trained nurses diffuse instruction in these three ways with durable results, as well as bring immediate aid and solace. Such a hospital would be an example of the characteristic Christian activity in altruistic works, and of the effective combination which has been made in the Occident during the past hundred years between Christian good will and the truth finding forces of modern science. It is this combination which during three generations has been gradually transforming Occidental society. Although this combination has borne admirable fruit in many Occidental professions and callings, it is in the medical profession, in medical and surgical practice, and in preventive medicine, that it has wrought the most beneficent works in both Europe and America during the past hundred years. All these physical and spiritual results ought to be transferred to the Orient; and an effective way of promoting that transfer would be to maintain an American hospital of the best sort in the educational center of China. With the hospital should be associated the usual laboratories for diagnosis and research. (See Appendix II.)

The Protestant Missions in China

In Tientsin I saw more of the work of the Protestant missions in China than in any other city. No fair-minded observer can look at their work as now conducted without feeling the highest respect for the men and women who do it on the spot, and for the Christian good will in the Occident which supports it.

The Protestant missions keep before the Chinese people good examples of the Christian family life; they show to all the Chinese people who come within their influence, young and old, rich and poor, fine types of Christian manhood and womanhood; and they perfectly illustrate in practical ways the Christian doctrine of universal brotherhood, of a love which transcends the family and embraces humanity. As a rule, the missionaries, both men and women, learn to speak some Chinese dialect, and become intimately acquainted with Chinese manners and customs, and with the workings of the Chinese mind. Other foreigners resident in China are often profoundly ignorant of everything Chinese. The missionaries are generally well informed. They teach Chinese children good Occidental literature, both religious and secular. They teach exact weighing and measuring, and accuracy in the use of numbers, subjects in which the Chinese are curiously deficient. They teach the inductive method through some elementary science and the household arts; and they teach out-of-door sports and the elements of personal hygiene. Since the European and American mission boards have provided some of their missions with medical missionaries, the missions thus strengthened have been enabled to answer in the most effective way the question of a certain lawyer to Jesus, "Who is my neighbor?" They have not passed by on the other side, like the priest and the Levite, but have showed mercy to the injured and the diseased. They have done exactly what Jesus told the lawyer to do,—"Go and *do* thou likewise"; and this doing has accomplished quite as much for the propagation of Christianity as the preaching and the teaching by missionaries. It is apparently impossible to make Orientals take an interest in the dogmas which have had such great importance in the history of Christianity in Europe; but they are quite capable of inferring the value of Christianity from the practical beneficence of Christians in the family and in society. It is the missionaries who have kept before the Chinese the good works of Christianity. Without them, the Chinese would have been left to infer the moral value of Christianity from the outrageous conduct of the Christian governments toward China during the past hundred and fifty years, from the brutalities of Christian soldiers and sailors in time of war, from the alcoholism of the white races as it is seen in Chinese ports, and from the commercialized vices which the white races practise in China. Against all these influences adverse to Christianity on the Chinese mind the missionaries have had to contend; and it is a miracle that they have won so large a measure of success.

During my residence at Tientsin I made two visits to Peking, one of ten days and one of four days, enjoying on both occasions the hospitality of the American Minister and Mrs. Calhoun at the American Legation. With the kind assistance of Mr. and Mrs. Calhoun, I had opportunities to meet most of the other diplomats at Peking, the leading missionaries and teachers, the officers of the American garrison, and the staff of the Legation. The greater part of my time, however, was given to making public addresses, visiting institutions of education, and talking privately with Chinese officials and professional men.

The Difficulties of the Provisional Government

It was in Peking that I arrived at a clear perception of the immense difficulties which the Provisional Government of China had to face, and also of the strength of the forces which make for Chinese unity. The difficulties of the new government had their origin in the fact that the Manchu Empire was no government at all in the modern sense. It did nothing for the public welfare, organized no national force, and no national system of education, and it created no stable, trustworthy public revenue for the central government. The Republic found in China no common language, no school system, no uniform system of weights and measures, no national currency, no common roads, only about five thousand miles of railroad in operation, and no revenue system except the Imperial Customs, the product of which was all devoted to the payment of interest on loans which the Chinese Empire had been forced to contract to pay indemnities to Western Powers, and the war expenses of those Powers in and against China. The northern provinces of China had somewhat different commercial and industrial interests from those of the south and the west. The Republic inherited from the Empire no body of national civil servants trained to conduct on modern principles the proper administrative departments of a government for the people. The different provinces had long been accustomed to a considerable degree of local self government, and had seldom felt any effective control from Peking. The Provisional Government had really been set up by several secret political societies whose plans and purposes were not identical, and which did not exist in the same strength in all parts of the country. Still another difficulty was created by the Provisional Government itself. Rashly perhaps, but inevitably, it early put an end to all the propitiatory and expiatory functions which the Emperor had performed for centuries on behalf of the Chinese people. In Peking stands in spacious grounds the most interesting and impressive structure in masonry, except the Great Wall, that one can see in China—the Temple of Heaven. It is a round, roofless mass of white cut stone with a great circular platform at the top which is provided with heavy stone balustrades, and is approached on four sides by three consecutive flights of nine steps each, with broad, slightly sloping landings between the flights—only twenty seven steps in all to the upper platform. Here the Emperor offered sacrifices twice a year to the Powers of Heaven, and prayed that the seed-times might be propitious and the harvests good, so that the labors of his people should be rewarded. There were no names on the Temple of Heaven, no idols, and no object to worship save the overarching heavens. The offerings were quite of the Hebrew type. Whole oxen were burnt in great metal baskets over broad wood fires, and many kinds of poultry in smaller furnaces. Papers on which prayers, praises, and thanksgivings were written were also burnt. All the animals used for sacrifice were carefully bred and raised in the Temple grounds, that each might be perfect of its kind and so acceptable to the Heavenly Powers. These ancient customs appealed strongly to the agricultural population of China; but the new Republican Government would have nothing to do with them. The Temple and its grounds are no longer a sacred preserve; and when I asked Mr. Tong Shao Yi if it would not be possible, when China got a duly elected President under a permanent constitution, to use the Temple of Heaven as a solemn place for administering to the President his oath of office, he replied that the new government could have nothing whatever to do with the old superstitions. As yet, however, the Republic has done nothing to discountenance the one religious conception which seems to be common to all China—the veneration of ancestors, a universal Oriental sentiment from Judea to Japan which has proved to be one of the prime sources in the East of national strength and endurance.

The Sentiments Which Make for Chinese Unity

Against these formidable difficulties, what forces could the Provisional Government bring to bear to unify China, and construct a strong, stable government for the eighteen federated provinces? These forces were only sentiments; but they were just such sentiments as have brought into being on other continents firm and enduring governments. The first was the sentiment of Chinese nationality; the second was the objection to an alien government, that of the Manchus, which was only a sham government; and the third was the sentiment of common resistance to the aggressions which the Western Powers had been committing for a hundred and fifty years on Chinese soil.

The sentiment of nationality is vast, vague, and hard to define; but the history of Europe and America is full of instances of its tremendous potency. It does not seem to need a common language, or a pure race, or a smooth blend of somewhat different races, or the same climate, or identity of the sources of livelihood. It is not necessarily based on similar histories, common traditions, or even the same religion. If we may judge from European and American experience, the sentiment of nationality is based on similar social standards or needs, on common ideals, on like passions good and bad, on a love of independence and liberty, on a preference for a large, comprehensive governmental unit over a small one, and on the desire to resist common dangers, wrongs, or aggressions from without. This last desire is very unifying the world over. Experience of misgovernment tends to unite the misgoverned, just as an earthquake, a destructive storm, a conflagration, or a flood always brings out in many of the sufferers a very practical brotherliness. Such seem to be the sources of the present development among the Chinese of a potent sentiment of nationality.

When several races live side by side on the same soil and form a community, it often happens that the ideals of one of these races dominate the development of all. This result has often been conspicuous in history, and is still exemplified in the present life of certain nations to which several different racial elements have contributed without being blended. The most essential element in the modern idea of nationality is identity of ideals, and of customs which are the offspring of ideals.

I have already mentioned in this report the growth in many regions of the world of the objection to alien government as such. It appears on a small scale and a large, in barbarous and semi-barbarous countries, and in countries which have long been civilized. It may be successfully repressed for long periods, though recognized. It may be long concealed by multitudes who feel it hotly; but it tends more and more throughout the world to break out at last, and win the day.

The motive of resistance to foreign oppression works wonders toward the formation of new national units, as has been forcibly illustrated in Europe during the past year. All China has had such bitter experience of oppression and robbery on the part of Western nations, that she inevitably possesses a strong unifying force in this common sense of unjust suffering.

A Strong National Government to be the Work of Many Years

The Republic has not yet been able to put into operation the obvious material means of unifying China; for the Republic has not had the money which the necessary measures must cost. A common language is the first unifying means; but from twenty to thirty years will be needed in order to diffuse throughout China among the children and young people a common speech. A common system of taxation is necessary; but now each province has its own methods of levying and collecting taxes; and these local taxes are not levied everywhere on the same objects or at the same rates on similar objects. To organize a uniform system of taxation for the benefit of the central government and to enforce it all over China will be a work of time and patience. The building of railroads on a great scale would contribute to the unification of the vast country, just as it has done in the United States; but how build them? Only by borrowing vast sums of money from the Western nations, and creating within Chinese territory vast supplies of rails, ties, cement, and crushed stone. Convenient and adequate sources of such materials are not yet discovered and developed. After the railroads must come the construction of innumerable common roads, before the productive capacity of the land can be developed, and the comfort of the rural population sensibly increased. All these great operations need time, patience, and an established public credit. China needs also new laws and a new legal administration. For all these works the country needs a government strong enough to preserve internal order, and to enable the entire population to devote itself to productive labor on the land, and in the mines, quarries, and factories. It took the American people thirteen years, from 1776 to 1789, to organize a strong national government out of the thirteen colonies; and yet the Americans were a comparatively homogeneous people having a common language and a common religion. China will need at least as long a period of reconstruction; and the Western world ought to stand by China with patience, forbearance, and hope, while she struggles with her tremendous social, industrial, and political problems.

The success of Japan in imitating selected Occidental methods in government and industries has had a strong effect on the Chinese. They have been roused and stimulated by seeing a neighboring Oriental race, close beside them, suddenly becoming a strong force in the broad world, in the West as well as in the East. That example has stirred deeply all the Oriental peoples, and has shown them that the Oriental races are capable of winning all the control over nature which the Occidental peoples possess, and of exercising all the truth finding powers which the Occidental nations have developed. The influence of Japan's example on China was much strengthened by the humiliating defeat which Japan inflicted on China during the recent war between those two countries,—a humiliation for which the Imperial Government and its most experienced foreign adviser, Sir Robert Hart, were utterly unprepared.

The hope that the Western Powers now encamped on Chinese soil will accept the doctrine that the creation of a strong central government is for the common interest not of the Chinese alone, but of all the powers, has been growing stronger ever since the revolution broke out. The division of China among the neighboring powers apparently looks less and less attractive to Great Britain, France, Russia, and Japan, and decidedly unattractive to Germany and the United States. The policy of the "open door," on the other hand, looks always more and more attractive to the trading nations; because it offers an open competition in the entire field, a privilege which would probably be lost forever if China were to be divided among Japan, Russia, France, and Great Britain. This trading privilege seems to be obtainable without cost through the policy of the "open door"; whereas the direct and indirect cost of maintaining an "imperial possession" or a "sphere of influence" looks as if it were going to increase.

The Value of the Chinese Markets

There is an obvious reason why the Chinese market should be scrambled for by all the Western manufacturing nations. Here is an immense population which does not possess any of the comforts of life that the Western peoples have long enjoyed. In China there is no household comfort, not even in the palaces, no comfortable furniture and bedding, no modern tools, no new hats and gowns every six months, and no luxuries like wines, beer, and tobacco. The population offers an immense field to the Western purveyors of comforts, good tools, implements, and machinery, the useful domestic animals, and the luxuries which in Western countries are within the reach of the great majority of the population, as well as the luxuries which only the rich can enjoy. The Chinese have never had any of these things; but they readily take to them, and would buy them all if they had the money. Hence the value of the Chinese market in the eyes of all the Western nations; hence the intelligent interest of all the Western nations in building up the Chinese producers, and giving them a government which will develop the public wealth of China. While I was in China, the British and American Tobacco Company was giving a demonstration on a large scale of the value to be developed in the Chinese market by the stimulation of new wants and desires. The Company was sending wagons and porters all through China, giving away cigarettes by the million in the towns and villages of the interior, and following up this gratuitous distribution with a supply of cheap cigarettes for sale. It was understood that this expensive procedure had been followed by a rewarding increase in the sales of cigarettes in China.

An American Free Public Library at Peking

Not long after I arrived in Tientsin I had an interview with four gentlemen, three Chinese and one American, who were concerned with educational institutions there established, and had been encouraged by an imperfect report of a speech I made at Shanghai to offer me some suggestions as to useful work which the Carnegie Endowment for International Peace might undertake in China. From this interview and some subsequent conversations there resulted a memorial (See Appendix III) to the Trustees of the Carnegie Endowment for International Peace, proposing that the Endowment establish at Peking a free public library on the American plan, to be built and carried on under the direction of the Endowment, but with the ultimate intention of transferring it in due time to the Chinese Government or to a board of trustees resident in China. It was proposed that this Library should maintain at Peking a free reading room open day and evening, and a good collection of books on such subjects as agriculture, mining, the fundamental trades, economics, geography, commerce, sanitation, public works, the applied sciences, government, public administration, international law, and the judicial settlement of disputes between nations. It should also permit any book which has been in the library one year and does not belong to the reference collection to be borrowed for home use during a period not exceeding twenty days, provided the borrower, if living outside of Peking, pay the postage. It should also through a special officer select, translate, edit, and circulate leaflets and booklets containing useful information on any or all of the subjects above mentioned, the distribution being made gratuitously, first, to Chinese newspapers and periodicals, secondly, to educational institutions, thirdly, to appropriate government officials, and fourthly, to private persons on request.

The memorial urged that this free library be placed in Peking, where many office-holders and candidates for office will always be living, where several important educational institutions already exist, and more are likely to be created, and where the Legations and the headquarters of press correspondents are established. This memorial was signed by many influential men, including three members of the Cabinet, a large group of Chinese graduates of American institutions, and Chinese gentlemen connected with the press and with the bureaus of the present government.

The argument in favor of such action on the part of the Carnegie Endowment for International Peace is strong. Here is a method of maintaining intercourse between the Western nations and the Chinese nation, by bringing to the knowledge of the educated Chinese the Western books, journals, and magazines relating to those subjects which the educated Chinese need to appropriate year after year and use for the benefit of their country. The influence of such a library would not be momentary, but enduring. It would take first effect on Chinese young men who had been educated abroad and had acquired some European language; but it would also provide a powerful means of influence on Chinese who had never studied out of China, and who knew no language but Chinese. It would provide an effectual means of intercourse between the East and the West; and it would enable the young men who had got to work in China after receiving a Western education to keep themselves well informed in the Western professional subjects through which they were earning their livelihood in China. It has often been observed that Chinese students returning from the Occident with a good knowledge of their respective subjects find it very difficult to keep themselves informed as to the advances later made among Western nations in the scientific, economic, and governmental subjects. Such a library would have to be conducted for a generation by American librarians, to be appointed and paid by the Carnegie Endowment.

It may be confidently assumed that the Chinese government would give an adequate lot of land as the site of the proposed building; for there are large areas of land in Peking which were formerly reserved for the Imperial family and clan, and will now revert to the government. The lot should be large enough to give plenty of light and air, and space for additions to the building.

The building need not be large at present, but should be of brick and steel construction throughout, and should represent in all respects the best type of American fire proof library construction. A stack capacity of from two hundred thousand to three hundred thousand volumes would be ample, and a reading room for a hundred persons would be sufficient. A building designed to cost a hundred and fifty thousand dollars gold ($150,000) in the United States, with heating apparatus, plumbing, and all furniture included in that cost, would be sufficient; for that sum would procure in China a building with fifty per cent more cubical contents than it would produce in the United States.

Books to the value of about thirty thousand dollars ($30,000) should be bought at the outset; and thereafter the annual cost of carrying on the library would be from twenty-five to thirty thousand dollars ($25,000 to $30,000). This estimate is based on present (1912) prices and costs of living in Peking. (For details see Appendix III.) If this estimate of annual expenditure seems small, it should be noticed that the memorial does not request that the library be a complete representation of all branches of knowledge. The great subjects of languages, literature, history, theology, philosophy, fine arts, and music are not mentioned.

The proposed library might well serve as a model for other Chinese provinces or cities. There is room in China for a dozen such institutions; and there is therefore a fair chance that the good work started in Peking by the Carnegie Endowment for International Peace may before long spread and be multiplied. Its influence would all be directed to strengthening the grasp of the Chinese on the applied sciences and the inductive method, and so to building up China as a strong, unified power, capable of keeping order at home, repelling aggression from without, executing the needful works of conservancy and sanitation, and increasing the national wealth and the well-being of all the people.

The Six Powers Loan to China

While I was in Tientsin and Peking the loan question was in active debate between the associated group of bankers, backed by the Six Powers, and the Republican authorities at Peking. The bankers were endeavoring to incorporate among the conditions of the loan a provision that the expenditure of the money borrowed should be supervised by foreign agents, and that the accounting should also be in foreign hands. The Chinese were resisting these conditions. Both parties agreed that the largest sum proposed to be borrowed would not support the government more than eighteen months; and both parties recognized that at least four fifths of the largest loan proposed would have to be used in paying off floating debts incurred partly by the Manchu Empire and partly by the revolutionists. The bankers insisted that the terms they offered the Chinese government were the only ones on which they could properly float the bonds in Europe and America; and each of the six governments supported its "nationals" in this view. The opposition of the Chinese government to the terms of the loan was entirely natural, since it grew out of their unfortunate experience with earlier loans, made after the war with Japan and after the Boxer insurrection; but they especially disliked the proposed supervision by foreign agents of the expenditure of the proceeds of the loan. The bankers maintained that unless the expenditure should be supervised by competent and trustworthy foreign agents, China would get nothing out of the loan. The Chinese officials, on the other hand, thought that Chinese agents could be found competent to expend the proceeds of the loan wisely, honestly, and productively. I found in conversation with members of the Cabinet that their minds and wills halted between two opinions. On the one hand, the educated Chinese generally have a certain complacency with regard to their own capacity for managing difficult and novel undertakings; but on the other hand, when they themselves are not involved they admit that China has not produced a class of officials competent for those departments of government administration which depend on the applied sciences. The members of the Cabinet with whom I talked admitted frankly that they were unable to man their own departments with competent Chinese. They admitted that the only way to get the work of the government properly done during the next ten years was to employ a considerable number of foreign experts; but almost in the same breath they would say that they could not venture to recommend that foreign experts should be employed immediately in their own bureaus, lest this action should give offense to their constituencies, the secret societies which had organized the revolution. They also urged that the experience of the Chinese had been very unfortunate with experts recommended to the Manchu government by Western governments, that many persons so recommended had proved not to be experts in their several lines and not to be trustworthy, and that the experts so appointed had continued to serve the foreign governments or foreign corporations to whom they owed their appointments, rather than the Chinese government in whose pay they were. They maintained that these objections held against foreign experts employed in industrial and transportation enterprises in China as well as against experts employed by the Chinese government. They maintained that foreign experts ought to be employed by the Chinese government itself without the intervention of any foreign government, and should be wholly devoted to the service of China; but they added that they did not know how to find such experts. They alleged that even Chinese gentlemen educated in Europe or America could not judge the character and capacity of a European or an American by his aspect and speech, and that they were not in position to conduct themselves careful inquiries into the antecedents of experts proposed for Chinese employment. These views were repeatedly expressed to me during my stay at Peking near the end of April.

The Conditions of Successful Borrowing by China

At a public banquet given on April 20, 1912, by the American College Club—a club consisting of Chinese and American graduates of colleges,—I had the privilege of listening to instructive speeches on the political and financial situation and foreign affairs by S. K. Alfred Sze, President of the Board of Communications, and Colonel Tsai Ting Kan, secretary and interpreter to President Yuan Shih Kai, Mr. Sze holding one of the most important posts in the new government, and Colonel Tsai being always near the Provisional President of the Republic. Both these gentlemen speak and write admirable English.

Through repeated conversations with Mr. Sze at Peking while he was Secretary for Communications and at Tientsin after he had retired, I verified the impressions I had received earlier concerning the grave difficulties under which the Provisional Government was laboring. On April 22 Colonel Tsai called on me at the private house of a mutual friend, and we talked freely together concerning the political and financial situation. I urged that the new government must have money; and inasmuch as it has at present no considerable revenue, it must borrow money for immediate use; that, inasmuch as it has no proper credit in Western financial markets, it is able to borrow only on crippling terms and by pawning some of its resources, developed or prospective; that China must borrow from Occidental peoples who alone have accumulated savings to lend; and that to enable China to borrow on open proposals in the markets of the world the Chinese government must win the confidence of the Western peoples that have money to lend.

To this end of successful borrowing on reasonable terms, two measures are essential, (1) the central government must obtain by methods of taxation that have approved themselves to Western scholars and statesmen a sure and ample income; (2) this income must be expended honestly and effectively on objects and in methods which have proved themselves good in Western governmental administration. The pressing problem then is—how can these two measures be put into effect with due regard to the honor and future independence of China? It is not reasonable to expect that the existing Chinese official class can furnish men competent to set up a new system of taxation, collect a stable revenue, and then spend that revenue effectively in the ways which have proved to be good in European and American experience. Foreign advisers must obviously be procured, and given authority enough to convince Western capitalists and governments that an adequate national income is to be secured, and that it is to be spent in a modern, scientific way. Having learnt that the Provisional Republican Government felt great difficulty, first, in selecting foreigners by its own unaided action, and secondly, in accepting them on the nomination of foreign governments, I suggested that the Trustees of the Carnegie Endowment for International Peace constitute a body competent to nominate to the Chinese Government advisers on many subjects; because it is a permanent, impartial, disinterested, and respected organization, which, though composed exclusively of Americans, has a broad acquaintance with scholars and experts of all nationalities. At the close of a long conversation, Colonel Tsai asked leave to translate into Chinese a memorandum I had with me in which the above points were concisely stated. He translated it on the spot, and assured me that he would bring it to the attention of the Premier and the President.

On April 25 I had another opportunity for conversation with Mr. Tong Shao Yi—at the ceremony of laying the corner stone of a new building for the Young Men's Christian Association of Peking, a building given by Mr. John

Wanamaker. At this ceremony the Premier, who is not a Christian, spread the mortar under the corner stone with his own hands, in the face of a large assemblage of Chinese, an act which illustrated forcibly the extraordinary departure already effected by the Republic from the ancient practice of Chinese scholars to abstain from every form of manual labor except writing. On the next day at a luncheon given by the Prime Minister to me and many members of the President's Cabinet, I had long conversations with Mr. Tong and other secretaries, mainly on the governmental and educational affairs of the Republic; and after the luncheon the Premier took me to an interview with President Yuan Shih Kai, the only other person present being Colonel Tsai, the President's interpreter. At this interview the conversation related exclusively to the difficulties under which the Republic was laboring, and to the best methods of procuring foreign advisers, Mr. Tong remaining silent during the whole conversation. The difficulties about the employment of foreign advisers were of two sorts. On the Chinese side, it appeared that China had had in times past many unfortunate experiences in endeavoring to employ foreign experts, and that the experts selected by foreign governments were very apt to put the interest of their own governments and people before Chinese interests. It was made clear that China needed the services of many foreign experts, but that they must be experts who were primarily servants of the Chinese government, and not of their respective nationalities. I conveyed to the President my suggestion that the Carnegie Endowment for International Peace could be of service to his government in regard to the selection of experts. This interview with the President was conducted with no more ceremony than obtains at the White House, Washington, and with the same kind of courtesy.

The Selection of Foreign Experts

A few days later, when I had returned to Tientsin, I wrote a letter to Mr. Tong Shao Yi in which I stated at length the method of avoiding all these difficulties concerning the employment of foreign experts by the Chinese government, through resort to the Trustees of the Carnegie Endowment for International Peace as an impartial and permanent body competent to select foreign advisers for service under the government of China. (See Appendix IV.) This letter was delivered by messenger to Mr. Tong Shao Yi at his office in Peking; but a few weeks later Mr. Tong retired from the Cabinet and left Peking.

On hearing in July that Dr. George Ernest Morrison had been appointed Adviser on Foreign Affairs to President Yuan Shih Kai, I sent him a copy of my letter to Mr. Tong Shao Yi; and in the following January Colonel Tsai sent me through Minister Calhoun and the State Department, Washington, a cablegram requesting on behalf of the President that the Trustees of the Carnegie Endowment for International Peace nominate an American professor well qualified in constitutional law and possessing a special knowledge of the French

Constitution as an adviser to be attached to the Chinese committee entrusted with drafting China's republican constitution. The favorable action of the Trustees on this request was recorded some months ago in the minutes of meetings of the Trustees of the Endowment and of the Executive Committee. The professor selected, Professor Frank Johnson Goodnow of Columbia University, reached Peking early in April, 1913.

There can be no doubt that within the last twenty-five years, among her widespread people possessing little means of communication, China has developed in her educated class an intense feeling of nationality. The revolution has proved that this sentiment of the educated class is capable of being communicated to millions of the uneducated, and, indeed, has been. The Chinese have now a full sense of Oriental nationalism, as distinguished from Occidental. They have been roused by the sight of another Oriental race suddenly developing a tremendous force in the international world, and asserting its right to control by force Oriental regions which did not originally belong to it. In short, they have had before them the example of Japan. That example has stirred deeply all the Oriental peoples; and it is impossible to say now how far that influence will extend.

The Pure Race is the Best

The foreign visitor in China recognizes several types of face and figure in the population, yet does not see in these diversities any strong racial differences. The Chinese themselves count five races in China, and have therefore put five stripes of color into their new flag. These are, however, kindred races, closely allied in origin and history, and in external appearance. The Orient teaches the world that the pure race is the best, and that crosses between unlike races seldom turn out well. The cross between any Oriental stock and any European stock is regarded as unsuccessful throughout the Orient, the Eurasians being approved by neither of the two races from which they spring. Japan illustrates the value of a race kept pure. As already noted, wherever the Japanese go as colonizers, they keep their race pure. No European race has done that. On the contrary, the white race transported to the East has mixed with every native race it has encountered. It is the Oriental that has demonstrated the advantages of race purity. Not only are the Chinese people permeated with this spirit of nationality, they have also been imbued with a fervent sentiment of patriotism. This, too, has originated in China with the educated class, and particularly with the young men who in recent years have been educated partly in Europe, America, or Japan. I have never seen anywhere better evidence of a widespread, intense sentiment of patriotism than I saw in China.

Just Sympathy With the Revolution

For an American who has seen many changes of public feeling at home, has lived through a terrible civil war, and has seen several alien races coming into his own country by the million, it is impossible not to sympathize profoundly with the present huge efforts of the Chinese people. It is impossible for the visiting American with any experience in administration and its normal difficulties not to sympathize with the few hundred men who have taken their lives in their hands and risked their whole careers in trying to build up a free government in China. What American could fail to sympathize with men in such a dangerous position, trying to do this immense service to such a people? Yet during my stay in China I seldom met Occidentals long resident in the country in diplomatic, consular, commercial, or industrial positions, who manifested genuine sympathy with the revolution, or any hopeful belief in the possibility of creating a free government in China. It seemed to me that this lack of sympathy and hope was partly due to the fact that most foreigners in China live there for years without making the acquaintance of a single Chinese lady or gentleman. The merchant may conduct for many years a successful and widespread business in China without knowing a word of the language, or making the acquaintance of any of his customers. In the clubs organized and resorted to by English, Americans, and other foreigners in the Chinese cities no Chinese person is eligible for membership. It is the missionaries, teachers, and other foreigners who labor in China with some philanthropic purpose, who really learn something about the Chinese. They get into real contact and friendly relations with the Chinese, both educated and uneducated; while the foreign business men probably remain ignorant of Chinese conditions and qualities, and Chinese hopes and aspirations. The ground for holding to the hope that it may be possible to create a free government in China is that the Chinese deserve to be free, because they are industrious, frugal, fecund, enduring, and honest. China will need a long period of reconstruction, and the Western world ought to stand by China with patience, forbearance, and hope while she struggles with her tremendous social, industrial, and political problems. She needs at this moment the Chinese equivalents of Benjamin Franklin, George Washington, and Alexander Hamilton. May she find them!

My party left Tientsin on the evening of June 8 in a special car provided by the Government. We were accompanied by Dr. Wu Lien-Teh, an eminent physician and professor of medicine with whom I had already had many interviews in Tientsin. He was chairman of the Mukden Conference on the bubonic plague in 1912, and was Deputy Director of the Army Medical School in Tientsin. He was thoroughly acquainted with the numerous difficulties attending the introduction of Western medicine into China, and had been active in preparing a memorial which I was to carry home with me, asking for the establishment and maintenance in Tientsin of a first-class hospital under American direction. It was a journey of about twenty-one hours from Tientsin to Mukden, and all day on June 9 we were passing through a fertile country, every bit of which appeared to be under cultivation; but the cultivators seemed to be few. The world may get a great surprise when a real census of China is taken. A city in which almost all the buildings are only one story high inevitably occupies a large area; and when city streets are not more than eight or ten feet wide, they seem thronged even when only a moderate number of persons are passing through them. In the country the population crowds into villages of one-story huts; and these villages may be hidden from a passing train by even small undulations of the land. All day on June 9 we noticed that the number of people at the stations where the train stopped was small, as if the population living within easy reach of the stations were sparse. The number of the Chinese people is not known to the present government within a hundred million on either side of four hundred million.

The Chinese government maintains at Mukden a governor-general, with a considerable cabinet, a palace, and an appropriate retinue, although the actual control over Manchuria exercised by either Empire or Republic has been slight. We were cordially received by the Governor-General, and were entertained at luncheon by the Commissioner of Foreign Affairs. The government was so greatly alarmed by the terrible outbreak of pneumonic bubonic plague which occurred in Manchuria in 1911-12, that it continues to maintain, in the plague regions, hospitals of an elementary sort ready at all times to receive plague patients. When Dr. Wu parted from us at Mukden, he made a journey through the plague region as medical inspector for the Chinese government. The pneumonic form of bubonic plague is the most terrible pestilence that afflicts humanity. Every person attacked dies, and thus far no promising treatment for it has been found. The urgent problem has been to discover how the disease passes from one person to another, and on this point some progress has been made. It probably passes directly from man to man, and therefore its spread can be in some measure controlled by adequate precautions in approaching and handling plague patients. The coming of the plague into the Philippines and the Pacific States is of course much dreaded; and the Philippine government and the legislatures of California, Oregon, and Washington have been only prudent in making appropriations for the study of the plague itself in the East, and of the means of preventing its transmission from one country to another.

The South Manchurian Railway is conducted by a Japanese corporation, under an agreement with China which permits the Chinese government to buy back the railway with all its buildings and equipment at the end of a moderate term of years. It seems to be the present Japanese policy to spend unnecessarily large sums on the buildings and other constructions which directly or indirectly serve the road; so that it may be difficult, if not impossible, for China to buy back the whole establishment at the end of the Japanese possession.

A Glimpse of Korea

On June 11 we rode from Mukden to Seoul through portions of Manchuria and Korea, being escorted all the way by Mr. Otsaka, representing the railway, and Count Inouye, representing the Governor-General of Korea, and were called upon in our special car by Japanese officials, teachers in the service of the Japanese Department of Education, press agents, and American missionaries and teachers at each of the principal stations. The country through which the train passed was well cultivated and looked fertile; but as the crops were young and rain was falling, the aspect of the country may have been unusually favorable.

We passed through Korea at an interesting moment. More than a hundred Korean Christians had lately been thrown into prison, charged with conspiracy against the life of the Governor-General, Count Terauchi, an eminent Japanese soldier and statesman. The supposed conspirators were for the most part disciples of Presbyterian missionaries from the United States, and were supposed to have held meetings and hidden arms on mission premises. The preliminary inquiry into the conspiracy was conducted by the Japanese police in a mode which the Japanese adopted and adapted from French methods before the French Republic had modified the traditional French system. From the Korean point of view, the method adopted was arbitrary and cruel, being directed to procure confessions which under the circumstances were nearly sure to be untrue. The missionaries had emphatically denied complicity with the supposed conspiracy, and had not been disturbed by the Japanese police. The case was later tried before a Japanese tribunal in Korea, and a large majority of the persons arrested were convicted and sentenced; but there were no death sentences. On appeal to a higher court, the case was subsequently re-tried at great length in Tokyo, all the proceedings being published. Here, most of the sentences were cancelled and most of the prisoners discharged, a few being sentenced to moderate terms of imprisonment. The chief lessons to be drawn from this interesting case were that the Japanese preliminary inquiry before police authorities needed the same kind of modification which the French procedure had already received in France, and that Japan would be obliged to hold the Korean people by force until through popular education, the multiplication of means of communication and transportation, and the resulting improvement in the comfort, health, and wealth of the Korean people, the two races, which are not far apart in natural quality and capacity, are brought together in good will with the conviction that their interests are common both at home and abroad.

On June 12 I visited in Seoul some interesting schools and a hospital which the Japanese authorities have already established and put in good working order. At a trade school, where several trades were taught, I noticed that there was only one piece of machinery in use, a simple lathe for turning wood, and that there was no power for driving that lathe. Thereupon the gentlemen with me explained that the Japanese government had thought it best to teach only the hand processes in the trades which the school undertook to teach, inasmuch as the graduates of the school, going out into the Korean life, would not have at their disposal mechanical power of any description. The government had distinctly abstained on purpose from equipping the school with steam power and machines. This seemed a sensible conclusion in a poor country like Korea, which has very inadequate means of transportation and therefore no cheap fuel for developing mechanical power.

Korea is a strong case of the complete inadequacy of feeble, despotic government to modern needs. To meet the needs of dense populations which tend to crowd themselves into cities and large towns, the customs and practices of an Oriental despot, or of an Occidental imitator of Oriental despotism, are hopelessly incompetent. They never were competent, except for a diffused agricultural population, the mass of which was content to stagnate, if left alone.

The Relations Between Japan and the United States

At luncheon with Count Terauchi in his official house and his charming garden, I had my first conversation with a Japanese statesman of large experience. Inevitably the conversation turned much on the past and future relations between Japan and the United States. He expressed the gratitude which Japan has long felt towards America for opening Japan to intercourse with the Occident, and awakening the government and the feudal nobility from their centuries-long sleep in isolation. This sentiment is common among Japanese thinkers, and should be a firm foundation for permanent amicable relations between the two peoples. He also stated in clear terms his views about the supposed probability of war between Japan and the United States, views which were afterwards repeated to me many times by Japanese statesmen and political philosophers without a single dissentient voice. Count Terauchi said in effect, "There is no interest of Japan which could possibly be promoted by war with the United States, and no interest of the United States which could possibly be promoted by war with Japan. The United States is the best customer Japan has. The commercial and financial relationships between Japan and the United States are becoming closer and closer; and each party finds great advantage in these relations. War, therefore, between Japan and the United States is not to be thought of. It is in the highest degree improbable, and neither nation in determining its policies for the future need take into account the possibility of war between the two." Count Terauchi belongs to the military party in Japan, which advocates the maintenance of as strong an army and navy as the government's resources will permit it to maintain; but these forces are maintained for urgent reasons which have nothing whatever to do with the United States.

Japanese Courtesy

At the Governor-General's luncheon Mrs. Eliot and I saw for the first time in a Japanese home the admirable courtesy of the Japanese to each other and to strangers. We had often seen this characteristic courtesy in Cambridge, New York, and Washington, and had recently seen it in China at Peking; but Seoul gave us our first experience of this delightful quality in the Japanese on Japanese soil, or rather, on soil become Japanese. Japanese courtesy extends all through Japanese life. It sweetens the intercourse of rulers with ruled, of masters with servants and servants with masters, of all employers with their employes, of hosts with guests and guests with hosts. It penetrates into all the relations of life, being always both dignified and gentle. Age commands reverence, childhood tender affection, and youth an interested regard. It is inevitable that Occidental persons should seem to the Japanese more or less brusque, inconsiderate, and rough, if not rude; but Japanese courtesy to Occidentals leaves nothing to be desired. Japanese ladies and gentlemen who have had experience in Occidental society come to understand that the Occidental gentleman is as refined as the Oriental, though not so gracious, and that the Occidental lady is just as modest and delicate as a Japanese lady, though to them she may not seem so. There is one point of good manners in which the Japanese, especially Japanese ladies, excel,—they are admirable listeners, visibly giving perfect attention with eyes and ears, and in pose or attitude, to the person who is speaking to them. They differ from English and Americans engaged in social intercourse in one not unimportant respect,—they smile less easily while talking, and laugh but little. They sometimes therefore seem grave and solemn to an unnecessary degree at moments when good cheer, or even merriment, would be appropriate. They bow to each other profoundly, putting the trunk almost at right angles with the legs; so that the nod, or slight inclination of the body, which the Occidental makes seems to them an inadequate salutation; but they condone this Occidental verticality, or perhaps accept the will for the deed. In entertaining Europeans or Americans, Japanese hosts and hostesses think it polite to dress in European style, and serve European food and drink; but they still exhibit in their houses the traditional Japanese style of dressing tables and using flowers and plants for interior decoration.

Japanese people of all ranks seem to enjoy public speaking and prolonged conversation. Any Japanese audience may be confidently expected to sit patiently in an attitude of eager attention through hours of speech making, even when they do not understand the language of some of the speakers, and have to wait for an interpretation. This patient attention is with them a part of good manners; but it also illustrates their real liking for public exhortation and oratory. The Chinese exhibit the same quality.

In riding from Seoul to Fusan, on the southeastern coast of Korea, one receives the impression that although Korea may not be so fertile a country as southern Manchuria, it nevertheless has abundant agricultural resources, if by good government the Korean people can be developed into ambitious workmen and comfortable householders. Fusan is one of the most important Korean ports, because of its proximity to Japan. One of the first cares of the Japanese government on taking possession of Korea was to improve several of the Korean harbors for both military and commercial purposes. Fusan was one of the ports so improved. The crossing from Fusan to Shimonoseki, the opposite Japanese port, now takes about ten hours at night on a comfortable passenger steamer, a fact which forcibly illustrates the common opinion among Japanese statesmen that the possession of the Korean ports is essential to the safety of Japan.

From Fusan to Tokyo

At Fusan we were met by Baron Chokichi Kikkawa, the first Japanese to take the degree of Bachelor of Arts in Harvard College, all earlier Japanese graduates having taken the degree of Bachelor of Laws. Baron Kikkawa, who graduated in 1883, was a member of a committee appointed by the Harvard Club of Japan to make plans for the best use of all my time in Japan, to provide a guide or courier, and to keep one or more members of the committee in attendance on my party so long as we stayed in Japan. At Shimonoseki another member of the Committee, Mr. Otohiko Matsukata (A.B., Harvard, 1906), joined us. The plans prepared by this committee were capable of modification at any point, and were frequently modified in accordance with my desire to see places or persons which had not been included in the selections of the committee.

We saw only southern Japan, following the main railroad line from Shimonoseki to Tokyo, but making short excursions both to the north and to the south. Coming as we did from China and Korea, the country seemed to us very beautiful by contrast, highly diversified in crops, trees, and shrubs, and tidy in respect to buildings and highways. Our first stopping place was Miyajima, a lovely health and pleasure resort on the Inland Sea, which combines all the usual features of a Japanese pleasure resort, a temple well cared for in beautiful grounds, pleasant walks through groves and tasteful gardens, tea-houses, Japanese inns, and an excellent hotel for foreigners. Miyajima, like such resorts in all parts of the world, had also its little bazaar on the road from the inns to the temple, where excursionists could buy picture post-cards and the similar trifles which in all countries attract the unfastidious visitor who likes mementoes. Here we had our first sight of a Japanese temple, which attracted numerous worshippers and visitors. It was a great contrast to the Chinese Buddhist temples we had lately seen, being in good repair, well furnished, and neatly kept. The scenery of Miyajima is of the lovely sort, not grand or awesome, but gentle and beautiful, lending itself to the ready development by man of facilities for enjoying it. The people who were enjoying it when we were there were for the most part women and children of the well-to-do classes.

By a short excursion from Miyajima I visited my first Japanese normal school, and also had the pleasure of seeing a Japanese country-house, that of the Kikkawa family. The normal school visit was the first of a long series of visits to schools of all kinds, primary, secondary, technical, and normal, and colleges, professional schools, and universities, both government-supported and endowed. These visits were rapid, but generally adequate for getting a clear impression of the external characteristics of the establishments and of the aspect of the pupils or students, and of their teachers or professors. I was usually furnished with documents in English, either printed or typewritten, which contained the programs and regulations of the institutions visited; and at most of these interesting visits I was expected to make a few remarks, which of course had to be interpreted to the audience. The institutions visited in almost all instances could furnish an excellent interpreter from my English into Japanese. The visits differed from visits to American institutions of education in one respect,—tea was generally served, without regard to the time of day, before the visit could begin and often also at the close of the visit; and in many cases the taking of a large group photograph was a part of the proceedings, and now and then the planting of a tree or a vine was asked for, the summer weather being apparently no obstacle to successful planting. In general, the Japanese newspaper reporters are as keen as any of their American brethren in getting snap shots and interviews; and a surprising number of them speak English.

A series of such visits to Japanese institutions of education, together with an examination of the programs and regulations of the institutions visited, left me with some distinct impressions concerning the Japanese system of public instruction, impressions to which I gave public utterance in one of the last speeches I made before sailing for home.

The Japanese System of Public Instruction

The first impression which the Japanese system of public instruction makes on an American observer is that of the marvellous promptness and skill with which a modern Occidental system was introduced all over Japan in the course of about forty years. The system was adopted from Europe and America, with ingenious adaptations to Japanese conditions; but the execution of the work has been chiefly in Japanese hands, although a few foreigners were employed at first. The objects and methods of the instruction were as novel as the organization itself; and the entire people has now enjoyed for a generation the fruits of this most comprehensive system. The school privileges of Japanese children are decidedly superior to those of American children on the average, and illiteracy exists today in much smaller proportion in Japan than in the United States. Great Britain never adopted a law which could possibly be thought to provide popular education till after the Japanese restoration of 1868 had taken place. In several countries of Europe popular education is still encountering serious obstacles; for example, it is not gratuitous, or it is given in part by ecclesiastical bodies, or the appropriations of public money for the purposes of education are inadequate. The achievements of Japan, therefore, with regard to popular education have not come late in comparison with those of Western nations, and they have been remarkable as regards their scope and their prompt success.

Uniform Programs Well Enforced Lead to a Uniform or Averaged Product

Nevertheless, even a cursory survey of the existing institutions of education in Japan will reveal to an American experienced in educational administration serious defects and dangers. These defects and dangers are analogous to those which educators in the United States have been trying to remedy in American school and college procedure for the past fifty years. Governmental prescription in education, no matter whether it proceeds from the nation, a province or state, or a municipality, is apt to be too rigid, and to be content with uniform or averaged results. At the start the Japanese government was of course obliged to issue uniform programs for all grades of education, and to give instruction through inspectors and superintendents all over the country in the carrying out of these fixed programs which issued from a central bureau. Again, a government bureau is sure to develop an inelastic examination system covering a large area of instruction, with uniform questions prepared by the examination specialists and not by the teachers. The argument for economy supports governmental, uniform methods, for large classes cost less per head than small ones, and uniformity in teaching on a large scale costs much less than diversity. In education, however, from bottom to top uniformity is usually pernicious, the utmost possible individual diversity being the proper aim.

The Liberalizing Influence of Endowed Institutions

The Japanese Department of Education has not yet begun to struggle with these difficulties,—indeed is perhaps not fully aware that the best results in education are only to be attained through a large freedom for both teacher and pupil, resulting in the utmost diversity of individual attainment. The private and endowed schools and colleges of Japan have been, as is natural, far less rigid and less content with uniform prescriptions than the government institutions. In them there is more academic freedom for both teachers and pupils, and they are sure to exercise before long a liberalizing influence on the Department of Education and on all its methods and policies. The private and endowed schools and colleges of the United States have had a similar liberalizing influence. One of the most admirable demonstrations of the growth of public spirit in Japan is the endowment of universities which are entirely independent of the government, such as the Doshisha University at Kyoto, the Keio and

Waseda Universities and the Woman's University at Tokyo. The Japanese educators have been much influenced by German practices in primary and secondary schools; but they have not quite appreciated the freedom and range of choice among subjects and teachers which a German university student enjoys.

Sense Training in Japanese Schools

Another strong impression which the development of education in Japan produces is, that the programs of instruction, from the elementary schools through the universities, contain a much larger proportion of sense-training through nature study, laboratory work, field excursions, and exercises involving some manual skill, than is usually found in the corresponding American institutions. A larger proportion of time is allotted to scientific subjects and to drawing, both mechanical and free-hand, than is usual in America. I had never seen at home normal schools for women so well equipped for teaching science and household arts as those I saw in Japan. I had never at home seen it made a part of the regular duty of the teachers in rural schools to take the children on walks through fields and woods, the object being not exercise merely, but opportunity for the teachers to give instruction about plants, animals, the lay of the land, the brooks and ponds, and the various aspects of the sky. The Japanese have been so eager to master the inductive philosophy, and to seize on all the industrial and governmental results of Occidental applied science during the past hundred years, that they have provided better in their system of public education for training the senses and applying the inductive method to everyday affairs than the Occidental countries in which the method originated have done.

The Education of Women in Japan

Another interesting result of the sudden creation in Japan of an Occidental system of public instruction comprehending both boys and girls cannot but enlist the eager attention of any American observer. Through the incessant action of the government provisions for the education of girls and women, new conditions are being developed for the whole female sex. For example, the government is turning out from its normal schools every year hundreds of well trained young women, competent to give excellent instruction in the schools of Japan, and also to become the intelligent and helpful comrades of educated men; and the endowed Woman's University at Tokyo is educating women to a high degree in many subjects. The Japanese women educated in Occidental countries return home with ideas about the functions, influence, and happiness of women which are new in Japan. It is plain that this diffused education must in time work great changes in Japanese society, and particularly in the relation of men and women in marriage. The transition from the old customs to the new will be disturbing and perhaps painful; but every step on the way ought to be an improvement, and the ultimate issue, when embodied in legislation,' will give the strongest possible testimony to the worth and power of Japanese universal education. The happiness of the Japanese home will be greatly enhanced when Japanese law and custom accept Ralph Waldo Emerson's definition of marriage—"a tender and intimate relation of one to one."

Effects of the Factory System in Japan

On our deliberate journey towards Tokyo, we paused at Kyoto, Osaka, Nara, and Nikko. Kyoto, the ancient capital of Japan, is still the seat of many characteristic Japanese industries, among them the manufacture of fine porcelain, fine lacquer work, and admirable work in bronze and other metals. Osaka is the principal seat of the cotton industry, but also possesses other modern industries in considerable variety. There I visited some of the best factories of various kinds, and had ample opportunity to observe the ill effects on the ancient hand industries of Japan of the importation of the factory system, and the substitution of the production of a great number of cheap goods for a small number of precious ones. In the manufacture of porcelains, for example, Kyoto is capable of producing work which compares favorably with that of two hundred or five hundred years ago; but as a matter of fact the great mass of the product is comparatively coarse, cheap, and ugly, being intended for Occidental markets, and particularly for that of the United States. While the Japanese still produce rich brocades and fine silks, delicate in both texture and color, and artistic cotton fabrics of several sorts, the bulk of the textile products consists of ordinary goods wholly machine-made, calling for little skill in design, and meant for large markets in which prices are low. A factory system, using machinery to the utmost, minimizing expenditure on artistic design, and multiplying one design to thousands or millions of copies, is sure to have this degrading effect on any industry formerly carried on by hand work with the maximum amount of design in each individual piece. Nevertheless, the textile, metal, and porcelain industries of Japan are doing a good service to the world, because they are supplying at low prices articles of considerable merit to millions of people, who before this transformation of Japanese industry had no supplies of the sort, or at any rate, no supplies of equal merit.

When, however, one studies the condition of the operatives in the factory industries of Japan, one soon sees that these industries cannot long be carried on in the manner now prevailing. In well managed cotton mills in Japan employing thousands of operatives, for example, the following conditions of labor exist:—The mills are run continuously night and day. The working force is divided into the day section and the night section; each section labors twelve hours, with three intervals along the twelve hours amounting together to forty or sometimes fifty minutes; and the night and day sections change places once a week. The girls and young women who constitute the great majority of the operatives lodge and eat in barracks within the mill's grounds, and very seldom go outside of those grounds. Their food is such as they like, and is carefully prepared and properly served. They sleep on the matted floors of large bare chambers, each girl having a quilt and other bedclothing of her own which she herself spreads on the floor when it is time to go to bed, and rolls up and puts into a cupboard or on a shelf when her sleeping period is over. The same large chambers serve the two working sections, and are therefore constantly occupied. Runners for each factory are constantly passing through the Japanese villages, recruiting girls and young women for this employment. The operatives generally engage for a period of three years; but it is unusual for a young woman to remain at the work more than one year, because the life soon tells on her health, spirits, and efficiency. She then leaves the mill, and returns to her native village with a small amount of cash, which facilitates her marriage. The employes are therefore constantly changing, new women coming in to take the places of those who retire. The newcomers quickly acquire the eye and finger skill required for the work of the mills, this skill sometimes being considerable, particularly in the silk industry.

The experience of the past twenty years has proved that it is possible to carry on factories on these terms; but it has also proved that the method is inexpedient for the population as a whole. It is too destructive of health and vigor, and does not develop a class of operatives who can maintain their health, increase their skill, and remain long in the service of the employing company. Recognizing these facts, the government has made ready a law regulating the conditions of labor in the factory industries; but it has postponed for several years the execution of the law, in order that manufacturers may have time to adjust their works to the new labor conditions.

Japanese competition with the factory industries of other countries is not likely to last in its present form; because the costs of production must inevitably increase in Japan in greater proportion than in the countries with which Japan is now competing. Not only will the labor cost increase, but the cost of living also. Indeed, the cost of living has already increased in Japan to a degree which seriously disturbs both the government and the people. The anxieties of the government on this subject are the greater, because it is difficult to see how the industries of the people can bear heavier rates of taxation than are now in use. The government is in great need of more money for civil as well as military uses; but it is hard to see how either agricultural holdings or industrial enterprises can be made to yield more revenue to the government than they now yield.

Japanese Temples and Shrines

At Miyajima, Nara, and Nikko, lovely pleasure resorts, we saw interesting temples and shrines at which there was a considerable popular attendance; and at Kyoto we lived for several days in a beautiful villa adjoining the grounds of a temple at which a festival of some sort was proceeding. All these temples and shrines had beautiful surroundings of garden and grove, and all had some attractive objects of interest beside the shrine itself, as, for instance, an immense image of Buddha and a great herd of tame deer at Nara, and the bridge at Nikko built for the Emperor to pass over alone on his occasional visits, no other use being ever made of it, since there was a much larger and more substantial highway bridge within two hundred feet. At all these shrines we saw the ordinary approach of the worshippers, and their ordinary acts of worship or petition. We saw the individual Buddhist worshipper bringing a single flower as an offering to the shrine, and the petitioner who cast a cent or two into the receiving box, put in his petition on a printed or written slip of paper, and rang with vigor a large bell suspended over his head, to attract the immediate attention of the deity. We saw the simple process of acquiring a prophecy concerning one's future, by making a brief statement of the thing desired to a youthful attendant, who drew a stick bearing a number from out a large bundle of such sticks, and then handed the inquirer a printed prophecy taken from a pigeonhole bearing the same number as the stick. There were many pigeonholes; but the selection of the particular prophecy was visibly determined entirely by lot, and all the life-prophecies were in print. We saw again the highly individualistic quality of the Buddhist worship, as we had seen it in Ceylon, each worshipper approaching the shrine alone, or in a row or file if there were many worshippers arriving at the same moment, making silently whatever petition he had in mind, and giving place to the next. There was no common prayer, no exhortation addressed to a congregation, no singing together. All day long and every day these processes went on, there being no concentration of auditors on any seventh day or first day of the week, although the visiting throng was greater on a festival day. A short service, comprising recitation of sacred sentences and many changes of posture—standing, kneeling, sitting, and touching the ground with the forehead—can be obtained on short notice by one or more persons who are prepared to pay a small fee, just as in the Roman Catholic Church a mass may be procured by an individual or a few individuals for a price. When on a festival day known or announced beforehand unusual crowds resort to a temple or shrine, other performances or spectacles interesting to the population will be supplied near the temple grounds, and there will be many temporary booths or tents wherein food and drink are sold.

The Maintenance of Religious Observances

The visitor or tourist who looks casually at many temples and shrines, and watches for a few moments at each the doings of the people who resort to them apparently with some religious motive or sentiment, is, of course, quite incompetent to decide how much effect such observances have on the national life, or on the conduct of the human beings who take part in the various rites and observances, just as a stranger of another religion would find it difficult to estimate the effect on personal conduct, or on the public affairs of Catholic countries, of attendance on the ritual and sacraments of the Roman Church. Such a visitor to Japan would soon learn, however, that the Japanese statesmen and thinkers are anxious about the national effects of the various religions which exist in the country, but in a condition of change or flux. The government recently spent a considerable sum of money on repairs to the immense statue of Buddha at Nara, and on the temple which encloses it. When a few years ago, the Emperor's bridge at Nikko was swept away by a flood in the narrow, rapid river it spans, the government immediately replaced it at the public expense. Every year the nation, by the Emperor or his representative and the army and navy, attend a simple but very affecting ceremony at the Shinto shrine in Tokyo which contains the paper rolls bearing the names of the soldiers from that district who were killed in the war with Russia. These young men died for their country before any children were born to them, and so have no children to venerate them. Therefore the nation must venerate them, by worshipping in the spring and fall of every year at the shrine where their names are kept in remembrance. Such acts look as if the government wished to maintain the ancient reverences.

The Toleration of All Religions in Japan

But other changes of practice indicate a disregard of former religious observances. For example, in the temple at Nikko is a Holy of Holies or interior shrine which is exquisitely finished in elaborate and delicate lacquer work, and contains many precious objects of art; it was formerly almost impossible for a foreign unbeliever to obtain access to this shrine; indeed, entrance to the shrine was prohibited to foreigners, and could be procured only by special favor and in secret. Now, any party of foreigners will be admitted at seven yen a head, a brief religious service being conducted by two or three priests before the shrine is entered. High military officials are concerned lest Japanese soldiers should become less devoted in battle, if the veneration in which the Emperor has been held by the common people should decline. Educated Japanese parents wonder if Christianity can give their children some strong motive towards purity and righteousness, more effectual than any Buddhism, Confucianism, or Shintoism has supplied. Japanese social reformers ask if there be in Christian activity on behalf of the public welfare any greater beneficent force than the precepts of passive Buddhism can be expected to supply. Japanese readers of modern history see that most of the defenses against the natural catastrophes of flood, drought, pestilences, and famine have been invented and applied in Christian countries, and that it is in Christian countries that man has learnt to use great natural forces for his own benefit. Hence the attitude of the Japanese government towards the religions which exist in the Empire is one of broadest toleration, without close alliance with any single religion. Shortly before my visit to Japan, the government called a conference of representatives of the various religions domiciled in Japan, the object of which was to procure the coöperation of all the religious bodies in promoting the veneration of the Emperor, each among its own people, by suitable observances consistent with the faith and practice of each religion. By many patriotic Japanese the death of the late Emperor was looked forward to with concern, because it was believed that his successor was not disposed to practise the same seclusion from the public gaze which the late Emperor practised. It is clear, then, that the religious condition of Japan is unstable, and that this instability may before long have grave political and social consequences.

Industrial Changes—Business Morality

The great industrial, financial, and social changes which have taken place in Japan since 1868 have produced a striking change in the business ethics of the commercial class. In Old Japan the trader was the lowest man in the social scale, below the agricultural laborer, and far below the mechanic or artisan. He was regarded as neither a producer nor a soldier, and being looked down upon by the rest of the population, his ethics in trade left much to be desired. As soon as the new government had abandoned the feudal system, established universal education, and brought the whole nation, instead of the distinct Samurai class, into military service, great pains were taken to raise in public estimation the commercial class, and to make it worthy of respect by inculcating the Occidental ideas of sanctity of contract, fair dealing, and commercial honor. Several of the principal families of feudal times went into business; and the government has taken pains to confer titles and orders on eminent business men. In these direct ways, and through the indirect effect of modern means of communication and of expanding commerce at home and abroad in teaching multitudes that successful business is founded on sound credit and mutual confidence between buyer and seller, there has come about so great an improvement in the average ethics of the commercial class, that the Japanese are now just as satisfactory people to trade with as the Chinese or the Americans. It is no longer true, as it may once have been, that an Occidental merchant might sell anything to a Chinese trader for future delivery, but nothing to a Japanese. No more precautions are needed in selling American oil, sewing machines, or structural iron all over Japan than are required in the United States. The Japanese merchant or banker has as good a standing in Japanese society as the American merchant or banker has in American society, his standing, like that of the American, being determined by his success, by the nature of his business, useful or harmful, and by the personal character his own business career has shown him to possess. All thinking Japanese know that the success of the expanding national industries, and particularly the permanent success of their foreign trade, are going to depend on the prevalence in the Japanese commercial class of as firm a business morality as prevails among Occidental nations.

Medical Science and Art in Japan

With the other applied sciences, the Japanese have imported the medical sciences and arts, and now practise them with extraordinary skill and ardor. The national and the provincial governments maintain hospitals, dispensaries, and sanitary service of the best quality; and Japanese surgery in particular is bold and, judged by its results, remarkably successful. Japanese preventive medicine has won many triumphs over contagious diseases, and has introduced into the army and navy, the hospitals both public and private, and the factory industries in some measure decided improvements in the popular diet. To be sure, foreign residents in Japan are seldom willing to avail themselves of a Japanese hospital; and Japanese physicians and surgeons do not welcome foreigners into their hospitals, because of considerable differences between Occidental and Oriental practices concerning diet and attendance; but for the Japanese population itself Japanese preventive medicine is energetic, skilful, and remarkably successful. There is, however, some difference between the Japanese state of mind about hospital and sanitary service and that of a Christian community. In health and disease matters the Japanese seem to be actuated by a desire to promote or maintain the efficiency of the community, more than by any humanitarian purpose to relieve suffering or show mercy. The Christian peoples are considerably influenced by the sentiment of brotherhood which the teachings of Jesus inspire. That sentiment does not seem to be so strong in the Japanese as in most Christian peoples, or at any rate, it does not prompt them to such active and continuous voluntary exertion. For example, lepers wander about Japan, and government and people alike seem indifferent to their sufferings. Tuberculosis in many forms is rife in Japan; but neither the government nor the medical profession is active in preventing its spread, or relieving its victims. Again, a Japanese hospital for poor patients, when utilized for giving clinical instruction, is not sure to make the interest of the patients its primary object, as is always the case in a well conducted American hospital. The number of hospitals in Japan for needy patients is altogether inadequate, although the great success of a few such hospitals has demonstrated the great usefulness of such institutions. The victims of incurable disease are not so tenderly cared for in Japan as they are in most Christian countries. These differences are apparently attributable to differences of religious belief and practice, and to the difference between the Buddhist saint and the modern Christian saint.

The Desires and Ambitions of the Japanese

All the enterprising Occidental nations are interested in determining accurately what the desires and ambitions of the Japanese people really are. The Japanese have proved by their achievements during the past forty-five years that as a race they possess fine physical, mental, and moral qualities. They possess in high degree intelligence, inventiveness, commercial and industrial enterprise, persistence, and the moral qualities which bring success in industries and commerce. They have learnt and put into practice all the Occidental methods of warfare on sea and land, and have proved that they can face in battle not only the yellow races, but the white. Are they then a dangerous or a safe addition to the world's group of national industrial and commercial competitors? Is their demonstrated strength dangerous to the peace of the world and to the white race? To answer these questions, it is indispensable to form a clear and just idea of Japanese desires and ambitions.

The Japanese are not a numerous people, for they number less than one-half the population of the United States. They are not a colonizing people. The Japanese government has had great difficulty in inducing Japanese to settle in Formosa, and at the present moment it has similar difficulties in Korea and Manchuria. To be sure, the climate of Formosa is too hot for the Japanese; but that of Korea and Manchuria resembles that of Japan. They are commercially adventurous, and will travel far and wide as pedlers, or in search of work and trade; but they are not colonists. They are a homing people, like the French. They have no more use for the Philippines than Americans have. If a Japanese trader makes money in a foreign country, he will take his family and his money back to Japan as soon as he can. They do not intermarry with women of any foreign race, affording thus a strong contrast to the white race when in foreign parts. The inexpedient crossing of unlike races will not be promoted by them in any part of the world.

The Japanese are not a warlike people, although within a few years they have waged two defensive wars, one with China and the other with Russia. They possess, indeed, admirable martial qualities, and make obedient, tough, and courageous soldiers in their country's service. Their fundamental motive in fighting, however, is not a natural love of it, such as is exhibited, or used to be exhibited, by some Occidental peoples, but a simple, profound loyalty to their country, and to the authoritative representatives of their country's power and will. In their intense patriotism pride, loyalty, and love are fused into a sentiment which completely dominates the private soldier, the officer, and the whole military and naval service. Still they are not an aggressive, conquering people; and they feel no motive for acquiring new territory, except near-by territory which they believe to be necessary to the security of their island empire.

The Domination of the Pacific

The Japanese are accused, chiefly by Occidental army and navy men, of intending to "dominate the Pacific"; but Japan has no such intention. All Japanese statesmen and political philosophers recognize the fact that Japan is, and always will be, unable to "dominate the Pacific." No one nation in the world could possibly control the Pacific Ocean. For that purpose a combination of at least four powers having strong navies would be necessary. Five or six powers combined, such, for example, as Great Britain, Germany, France, the United States, Japan, and Russia or Italy, could do it; and could at the same time dominate all the other oceans and seas. Such a group would possess ports and coaling stations on all the seas and oceans. It would be convenient, though not indispensable, if one strong South American government on the Atlantic coast and one on the Pacific coast joined the group. There are many who think a control of the oceans by such a combination would be desirable; because it would tend to remove some of the apprehensions which cause war and preparation for war, and to check in their early stages offenses committed or contemplated by one nation against another.

All Japanese leaders are fully aware that it would be impossible for either Japan or the United States to send an army of a hundred thousand men with their baggage, animals, stores, and munitions, across the Pacific Ocean in safety, although the fleet should be convoyed by scores of battleships and armored cruisers. The means of attack at night by almost invisible vessels on a wide-extended fleet in motion are quite adequate to arrest or destroy any such expedition, if the attacking force were even tolerably alert and vigorous. If by miracle such an army should effect a landing on either shore, it could achieve nothing significant, unless the first expedition should be immediately followed by a second and a third. The scale of modern warfare between nations is too large for such remote expeditions,—no matter what the resources of the nation that should be rash enough to attempt them.

International Peace is the Interest of Japan

Japan, being heavily burdened with debts incurred in carrying on her wars with China and Russia and making internal improvements, could not borrow the money necessary in these days for waging aggressive war on a large scale at a distance, although she might fight successfully on the defensive at or near home. That much she could doubtless do, as many other poor nations have done; but her financial condition is such that she will be prevented from engaging in offensive war for at least a generation to come. Moreover, all the capital which Japanese merchants, manufacturers, and financiers can possibly accumulate during the next thirty years, is urgently needed for the execution of public works and the expansion of industrial undertakings at home. The industrial and commercial interests of Japan require peace with all the other nations of the world. As Count Terauchi said to me at Seoul, "There is no interest of Japan which could possibly be promoted by war with the United States or any other nation; and conversely, there is no interest of the United States which could possibly be promoted by war with Japan." Such, as I have said before, was the opinion of every Japanese statesman and man of business with whom I talked in the summer of 1912; and many of these gentlemen said that they had never met any Japanese political or commercial leader who was not of that opinion. The entire commerce between Japan and the United States is for the mutual advantage of each country, and the United States is Japan's best customer. War between the two countries is not to be thought of; and to suppose that Japan would commit an act of aggression against the United States which would necessarily cause war is wholly unreasonable, fantastic, and foolish, —the product of a morbid and timorous imagination.

Japanese Labor and Capital Needed at Home

Japanese statesmen are not in favor of any extensive migrations of Japanese people to other lands. They want Japanese emigrants from their native islands to settle in neighboring Japanese territories. They hold that the Japanese home industries need all the labor the population can furnish. Japanese economists greatly prefer to the planting of Japanese capital or labor in foreign lands the recent methods of planting foreign capital in Japan. When an American corporation, which is conducting at home a successful industry, sells its patents and methods to a body of Japanese capitalists, and then takes a considerable portion of the stocks and bonds of the Japanese company, American capital finds a profitable investment, the Japanese laborers remain at home, and the product of Japanese industry is sold to advantage in the markets of the world. Japan wants foreign markets for its manufactured products. War, or any other action or event which interrupts commercial relations with other countries is adverse to Japanese interests.

The right state of mind of Americans towards Japan is one of hearty good will and cordial admiration. Japan should receive every privilege in the United States which the "most favored nation" possesses; and that is all Japan wants from the United States, except the respect due to its achievements, and to the physical, intellectual, and moral qualities which have made these achievements possible. All classes in Japan, the uneducated as well as the educated, the poor as well as the rich, are sensitive about being treated, or thought of, as if they were a backward, semi-civilized, untrustworthy people. They wish to be regarded as a worthy member of the family of civilized nations.

Appropriate Expenditures of Carnegie Endowment Income in Japan

I spent a fortnight in Tokyo, visiting the four universities situated at the capital, and various schools, hospitals, and missions. Many hospitalities and social attentions gave opportunities for interesting and instructive conversation. Here I learnt that an American free public library, similar to the one proposed for Peking, would be a welcome addition to the intellectual resources at home of the Japanese educated abroad, and would unquestionably promote the continuous friendly intercourse and exchange of ideas between Japan and the Occident. There, too, I found that a well endowed hospital for foreigners, under American direction, would be of great service to the foreign residents of Japan, China, and of the seaports where foreigners live as far south and west as Manila, Singapore, and Bangkok. A hospital for foreigners established at Tokyo would be available all the year round, and in summer would be a safe refuge for sick or wounded foreigners who inhabit the hotter cities to the south. At present, a foreigner living in any part of the Far East who is attacked by any disease which requires hospital treatment is obliged to contemplate a long journey to either Europe or America, in order to get competent treatment in a good climate. There are many cases for which so long a journey is dangerous, or dreadful, or even impossible. A first rate American hospital at Tokyo would add greatly to the sense of security of European and American families that are living in the Far East for business reasons, or because they are employed in diplomatic, consular, or missionary service, or in teaching. A memorial asking for the endowment and support of such a hospital, signed by representative persons in Tokyo, both Japanese and foreign, will be found in Appendix V.

It is characteristic of foreign service in the Far East, whether governmental or commercial, that the persons so employed remain but a short time in their Oriental stations, and are rapidly replaced. One of the reasons for the rapid shifting of the foreign population is the entire lack in the Far East of thoroughly good schools for the children of foreign residents. Parents are content to keep children in the Straits Settlement, Siam, China, the Philippines, or Japan, until they grow old enough to need first rate secondary schools; but when the children get to be twelve or fourteen years of age, it becomes a grave question whether they shall be sent to boarding schools in the United States or Europe, or the mother shall take the children home, leaving the father in the East, or the whole family shall abandon their post of service in the East, and return to the native land. If there were a thoroughly good secondary school at Tokyo, conducted by English, American, French, and German teachers, which would be a day school for residents of Tokyo and a boarding school for the children of residents of other places, the average stay of foreign families in the East would unquestionably be prolonged and the unhappy division of many families be prevented, to the advantage alike of the Oriental countries and of the Occidental governments, corporations, or societies in whose service the fathers of these families have enlisted. I should therefore regard it as a good use of some of the income of the Carnegie Endowment for International Peace to endow and support in part at Tokyo a good secondary school for the children of foreigners resident in the Far East. A memorial on this subject signed by representative persons living in Tokyo, both Japanese and foreign, will be found in Appendix VI. Some of the young graduates of such a school, who had learnt the language of the region where their parents live, might decide to enter commercial or government service in the country where they grew up,—to the advantage of international commerce, and friendship.

We sailed from Yokohama July 13 via San Francisco, but stopped a week at Hawaii to observe the condition of the numerous races that have been brought into the Islands as laborers, the state of the Island industries, and, if possible, the results of the interbreeding of the numerous races now inhabiting the Islands. The planters and the territorial government together have fostered, or actually paid for, the importation in considerable numbers of Portuguese, Japanese, Chinese, Porto Rican, and Korean laborers. Other European races have come of their own accord. The American contingent of the total population is decidedly smaller than any one of the following contingents,—Hawaiian, part-Hawaiian, Portuguese, Japanese, and Chinese.

The Schools in Hawaii

All the white races or nationalities and the Chinese have mixed with the Hawaiian stock; so that the number of school children called "part-Hawaiian" is nearly equal to the number called Hawaiian, and is nearly four times the number of children called American. Nearly one third of the children in the public and private schools of Hawaii are Japanese, the pure Japanese children being almost as numerous as the Hawaiian, the part-Hawaiian, and the Americans added together. In the year 1911-12 nearly thirty thousand pupils attended the public and private schools of the Territory. Of the nine hundred teachers nearly one half were American. Of the rest, nearly three fifths were Hawaiian or part Hawaiian, the remainder being distributed among six different nationalities, the Portuguese supplying the largest number contributed by any one of the six, namely, fifty one. In the Hawaiian schools pupils of European, Oriental, and Hawaiian extraction sit beside each other, study the same lessons, sing the same songs, and play on the same athletic teams. Nearly one half of the children in the public schools are enrolled in the first four grades, in which the English language and literature are the main subjects of instruction. Since 1896 the use of the English language has been compulsory in all schools. Two years later formal instruction in the Hawaiian language was finally discontinued. Since 1899 the public schools have been free schools.

It is to be observed concerning this extraordinary medley of schoolchildren, that all the races represented in Hawaii possess a good degree of intelligence, and are capable of profiting by a long continued training in school. Among them all there is no race that can fairly be called backward or barbarous. The part-Hawaiian contingent of children is the least vigorous contingent, but it is gentle and fairly intelligent. Every other race on the Island except the Japanese has intermarried freely with the Hawaiians; but the progeny of all these crosses, being put together in the successive censuses and the school reports under the title "Part-Hawaiian," it is not possible to trace the physiological effects of the different race admixtures.

Hawaiian Experience in Crossing Races

Although nearly six generations have been produced since white men first visited the Islands and the crossing with the Hawaiian race began, no accurate statistics concerning the interbreeding are obtainable, and very few family records have been kept with sufficient accuracy and completeness to make them instructive. The inquirer can get from the present inhabitants only general impressions concerning the results of the interbreeding, and these impressions are naturally colored in many cases by individual experience or temperament. The general impressions, however, seem to agree on a few points,—first, that the pure Hawaiian race has been rapidly and largely reduced in number, and will apparently cease to exist before long, in spite of universal education and the many agreeable qualities of the race; secondly, that no one of the many crosses of race which have taken place in the Islands has succeeded in producing a progeny of sound and durable quality; and thirdly, that the best cross the Islands have to show is that between the Chinese man and the Hawaiian woman; but opinions differ as to whether the merits of the progeny from this cross are due to the harmonious blending of the qualities of the two races, or to the fact that the Chinese man makes a better father in bringing up his children by an Hawaiian mother than any other male known to the Islands. The Chinese who marries an Hawaiian woman may be an excellent specimen of his race. The American, Englishman, or German who marries an Hawaiian woman is not so likely to be a favorable specimen of his race. On the whole, if exceptions be neglected, the best conclusion from the experience of the Islands seems to be tolerably clear, namely, that the pure race is the best, and that the crossing of unlike races is undesirable.

Two natural processes tend to confuse the issues of this remarkable experiment in interracial breeding. In the first place, in a large family of children born to parents of unlike races, some of the children will incline to resemble the father most, and some the mother. In the next generation the children who resembled the father may intermarry with his race, in which case their children will tend to revert to his type, or they may intermarry into the mother's race, with quite different results. The same will be true of the children who resembled the mother. Their children may tend strongly towards the mother's type. These part-Hawaiians may marry other part-Hawaiians, and the mixing so be extended and continued, with further dilution of the characteristic qualities of each of the original stocks. Feeble descendants of a crossed marriage may be extinguished in a generation or two, a fate which must have overtaken many part-Hawaiians, else the successive censuses of the Territory would show a larger increase in that portion of the population than has actually taken place.

It is highly desirable that the physiological effects of the large-scale experiments in the admixture of races which has taken place in the Islands should be carefully observed and recorded for the benefit of mankind; but this work would require the careful attention of many experts for many years, and the Territory is not likely to appropriate for such an inquiry the large sums of money it would inevitably cost. If, however, the ordinary vital statistics concerning births, deaths, and marriages shall be well kept in the Islands for a hundred years, with mention of the race in every item, some sound conclusions can probably be drawn at the end of that period.

The Labor Problem in Hawaii—Immigration and Importation

The heavy expenditures of the sugar planters and the territorial government on the importation of laborers have not been rewarded by complete success. A considerable number of Portuguese have been brought to the Islands in recent years, and latterly some Spaniards of the poorer sort; but no satisfactory method of keeping these laborers in the Territory has been contrived. They exhibit a tendency to cross over to the States, as soon as they have laid by a sufficient sum of money. The Portuguese also exhibit in Hawaii a disposition to abandon the earning of wages so soon as they have laid by enough money to enable them to hire a piece of ground and work it for themselves. The Portuguese, particularly the natives of the Azores, exhibit this tendency in every country to which they emigrate, notably in Bermuda and New England. The Japanese and Chinese have been admirable laborers in Hawaii, as they are everywhere; but they, too, desire to become proprietors themselves; and in Hawaii many of them have been enabled to do so, in spite of the fact that the principal industry of the Islands—the sugar industry—is one which requires capital and large use of costly machinery.

Of late years the Island agriculture has been more diversified than it formerly was, and every new crop that succeeds, like the pineapple crop, for example, improves the labor conditions of the Islands. Many of the large planters have learnt that the barrack system of housing laborers is undesirable, and that the way to secure a permanent, contented laboring force is to settle families on the estates, each family being provided with a cottage and a garden. The Chinese and Japanese who first came to the Islands brought too few women with them; but in recent years more and more women of these races have been brought to the Islands, with good results.

The Japanese colony in the Islands is large, numbering from seventy five to eighty thousand persons; and one of the most interesting problems which is to be worked out during the next thirty years is the problem of converting this Japanese population into contented and useful American citizens, weaned from their native land. Heretofore the successful Japanese in Hawaii have shown a strong tendency to send their children to Japan as soon as possible; but there are some signs that this tendency is diminishing in force. If the Japanese born in the Islands are given the American type of education, and all civil rights when they come of age, and if all employments are open to them, it may turn out that the Japanese will come to share completely the Christian civilization which the American missionaries introduced into the Sandwich Islands. To this end diversification of the Island industries, the continuous improvement of the schools and colleges of the Islands, and a greatly increased resort thither of American and European seekers for health and pleasure would strongly contribute.

Wars and preparations for war continue, because many of the causes of war in time past continue to exist. The Occidental peoples have for several centuries fought oftener and harder than the Oriental; and the Christianity which prevails among them has little, if any, tendency to prevent their fighting among themselves, sometimes with ferocity, or to prevent them from attacking non-Christian peoples, if they think it their interest to do so. The Eastern peoples, Far and Near, as has been already mentioned, will have some causes of their own for war; because in some important instances neither their geographical limits nor their governmental institutions are as yet settled. One Eastern people has recently acquired the whole of the Occidental art of war with its subsidiary sciences, and other Eastern peoples are on the way to the same acquisition. War will last until its causes are rooted out, and that extirpation will prove a slow and hard task. The Carnegie Endowment for International Peace is just entering, therefore, on labors which will last for generations. Its reliance must be on the slow-acting forces of education, sanitation, and conservation, on the promotion of mutual acquaintance and advantageous commercial intercourse with the resultant good will among nations, and on the steady, patient use of the civilizing agencies which humane democracy and applied science have invented and set at work within the past hundred years.

Profitable Expenditures for the Promotion of Peace

From the observations recorded in the above Report, certain inferences may be drawn concerning profitable expenditures for the promotion of international peace by the Division of Intercourse and Education of the Carnegie

Endowment for International Peace. It may be safely inferred that action in any of the following directions will bring nearer the coming of peace:—(1) Create or support agencies competent to reduce, relieve, or prevent so far as is each day possible, the wrongs, miseries, and illusions which have caused, and are still causing, wars. (2) Strengthen public opinion in favor of publicity in governmental and commercial transactions. (3) Suspect and probe all secrecies and hidings in the family, in industries, in legislation, and in administration. Oppressions and robberies are generally concocted in secret. It is one of the worst consequences of long continued and severe oppression, that the resistance to it and revolution must be nursed in secret. Inquire, bring light, and publish. (4) Cultivate in all nations trusteeship, public spirit, and the application of private money to public uses. (5) Create or foster, in addition to universal elementary education, permanent educational agencies such as libraries, hospitals, dispensaries, training schools for nurses, and technical and professional schools in countries which lack these instrumentalities. (6) Recognize frankly the present necessity of maintaining in all countries armed forces for protective duty against aggression from without, or disintegration from within. (7) Strengthen international public opinion in favor of an international naval force to secure peace and order on the seas, and a freedom that cannot be interrupted for water-borne commerce. (8) Foster those religious sentiments and those economic, industrial, and political principles which manifestly tend to purify and strengthen family life, and to secure liberty, domestic joys, public tranquillity, and the people's health, morality, and general well being.

CHARLES W. ELIOT.

APPENDIX I
The International Institute of China
LETTER OF DR. CHARLES W. ELIOT.

TIENTSIN, May 28, 1912.

DEAR DR. REID:

Your letter of May 21 was handed to me last evening and I hasten to reply to it.

The objects of the International Institute of China are closely akin to the objects of the Carnegie Endowment for International Peace, and you have been, for years, an effective pioneer in promoting those objects in China. Therefore, I think, the Trustees of the Carnegie Endowment might reasonably promote your work; but some practical considerations might deter them. Will you allow me to mention those considerations?

(1) The International Institute seems to be a personal creation, and its present efficiency seems to depend upon you alone. Now, the Trustees of the Carnegie Endowment would naturally prefer to aid an institution, which gave promise of permanency, or, at least was not dependent on the life of any individual.

(2) The Institute was originally incorporated in Hong Kong in 1905; later, it appears in Shanghai with a small plant; and now, in your letter of May 21, you state "It is my purpose to resume our work in the Capital, while continuing the work in Shanghai." Might not the Carnegie Trustees prefer a fixed or permanent center for the work of your Institute?

(3) Your request for an annual contribution of, from $7,500 to $10,000, to be used for salaries, would inevitably raise in the minds of the Trustees the question, for how many years their annual contribution might last. Competent assistants can rarely be secured for short terms of service, and in such work as yours, experience would add greatly to the value of assistants employed. Had you in mind a pledge for the Carnegie Trustees for a term of years? The letter you addressed to Secretary James Brown Scott on March 23, 1911, does not touch that point.

Have you received any reply to your communication of March 23, 1911? I do not remember to have heard your application mentioned at either of the meetings of the Trustees which were held before I left home; still, it may have been dealt with by the Executive Committee. Are you personally acquainted with Dr. Scott, and has he knowledge of the work you have done in China?

You will perceive from what I have written above, that I am thinking about the best way to further your application to the Carnegie Endowment for International Peace.

The application to the Trustees for a library in Peking has, I am told, been signed by a considerable number of influential Chinese, and by a small number of foreign residents; but as yet, I have not seen the list of signatures. The effort seemed to me to be an intelligent one and a well-directed one; but I have no idea whether it will commend itself to the Trustees of the Carnegie Endowment or not. If the proposed library should be established at Peking, the work of the library and of the International Institute will be coöperative, and each institution will help the other.

Kindly address your reply to me, care of The Hundredth Bank, Tokio, Japan.

I am, with great regard,

Very truly yours,

(Signed) CHARLES W. ELIOT.

Dr. Gilbert Reid.

LETTER OF REV. GILBERT REID, DIRECTOR.

INTERNATIONAL INSTITUTE,
290 Avenue Paul Brunat, Shanghai, China, June 12, 1912.

PRESIDENT CHARLES W. ELIOT.

DEAR SIR:

Your letter written from Tientsin under date of May 28 has been duly received. I thank you for bringing so clearly to my attention certain features of our organization, which may lay the Institute open to criticism. I now deal with the points brought forward in your letter.

(1) I know Dr. James Brown Scott quite well. He has shown his personal interest by becoming a member of the Institute. He has furthermore helped me by suggesting a possible criticism for me to answer.

(2) I have had no reply from the Executive Committee or Trustees, though Dr. Scott has acknowledged promptly all my letters. He wrote me that he would submit my application. I have this spring renewed the application.

(3) As to the Institute being my personal creation, I have nothing to say to the contrary; but it has got beyond the stage of creation. I first secured the coöperation of the former Imperial Government and officials. I next secured the coöperation of Chinese and foreign merchants and other men of standing who are "on the ground." I next secured legal incorporation, defining the responsibilities as resting with different parties or committees. I last of all have secured promised annual support in America for five persons. This is in addition to support obtained in China. I am still working for endowment, though some, like Cleveland H. Dodge, argue that more vitality is secured without an endowment. Should a little more help be forthcoming, I would feel that I could withdraw, if desirable, without injury to the work. With the help we now have, there is guaranteed permanency *on a small scale*. With more help, there would be guaranteed permanency *on a large scale*.

The International Institute appears to be dependent on me, because I have been its originator, but I am anxious to have the Institute so organized and developed that it not only will not be dependent on me, but will not *appear* to be.

In the line of peace and concord, there is no institution in China to be helped. For this reason I represented the International Institute at the American Peace Congress of last year, at the same session which heard Dr. Scott. While the Institute plans ways of helpfulness and uplift in many directions, it is yet true that Harmony is our corner-stone, and with the improvement of harmonious relations, there comes the true exhibition of universal peace.

(4) According to our charter, Shanghai is our headquarters. This refers especially to property. Our incorporation also permits branches. The Institute is named "The International Institute *of China.*" If Peking remains the capital, our efforts, both for peace and concord and the general cause of enlightment, should be concentrated there as well as Shanghai. To my mind, work in both of these places, with connections maintained at other centers, would lead the Carnegie Endowment to utilize our Institute and give it help, rather than induce them to ignore our claims.

(5) As to term of years for financial help, I have preferred to leave it to the Carnegie Trustees. I have been willing to rely on the help only so long as their agents in the Institute should give satisfaction. Certainly if the Institute is to get its peace workers of a competent kind from abroad, still more from America, it would be desirable to have a term of years, say, ten. I agree also that experience is to be desired. And here I would say, that if my own services should be wanted in this special branch, which attracts me as no other work, I stand ready to obey instructions. In that case I would hand over my duties as director in chief of the Institute, consisting of other things than peace, to some

one else, while I would concentrate on this one development, and report accordingly to the Carnegie Endowment. In my application, as you have observed, I made no mention of this, but at the same time I am conscious that I have had considerable experience in the basic principles of universal peace, in application to China.

As mentioned in my application, the objects of the International Institute have been, and are, in perfect harmony with the objects of the Carnegie Endowment. Such objects are fundamental to the plan of both.

In conclusion, may I ask you to bear in mind not only our desire for help from the Carnegie Endowment in the line of international peace, but my aim to secure an endowment of $500,000 to meet the salaries of fifteen Americans, devoted to all branches of enlightment, friendliness and development. This would mean a staff of workers forever and forever, exerting an influence on the whole of China, and also on all world-wide problems. With this secured, there could be no possible doubt as to the permanence of the International Institute of China. This particular request I made of Mr. Carnegie and Mr. Rockefeller, but without success. Should success come hereafter, it is almost certain that a similar number of workers could be secured in China and other countries, supported by their countrymen or governments. This is my ambition. Providence who has guided us hitherto, will yet lead us into larger usefulness with greater support from the generous-minded in all lands.

Thanking you for this opportunity to make clear my wishes, believe me, with expressions of esteem,

Yours very truly,

(Signed) GILBERT REID,
Director in Chief.

APPENDIX II
Memorial for the Endowment of a Hospital in China

TIENTSIN, CHINA, *August 1, 1912.*

To FREDERICK T. GATES, ESQ.,
26 Broadway, New York City, U. S. A.

SIR:

We, the undersigned, comprising medical practitioners, gentry, merchants and educators of North China, have the honour to submit to you the following memorial.

For years Tientsin has been the center of the educational, municipal and other movements started by Viceroy, now President, Yuan Shih Kai. Among institutions established, those for medical instruction and for the relief of the sick have taken a leading part; but unfortunately, owing partly to insufficiency of government funds and partly to the backwardness of the people, the hospitals so far established have not been able to cope with the large amount of work or to keep up with the march of modern medical science. The widespread suffering caused by the recent revolution has further accentuated the need of a well-equipped hospital, which will not only serve as a model for the rest of China, but will confer untold benefit upon thousands of sick Chinese and serve as a center where the medical students and local practitioners may witness the highest development of medical science as well as enable workers to pursue research on the many diseases peculiar to this country.

We believe that Tientsin is particularly fitted for this purpose, as, besides being the third seaport in China, it is the largest city in the north, which comprises the provinces of Chihli, Shansi, Shensi, Shantung, Honan, and Manchuria, with whose commerce and material progress it is largely associated. The medical institutions which have been established by the Government in Tientsin are:

1. The Peiyang Hospital founded by the late Viceroy Li Hung Chang about twenty years ago in conjunction with the Imperial Medical College. It has accommodation for forty patients.

2. The Tientsin City Hospital, established eight years ago by Viceroy Yuan Shih Kai in association with the Army Medical College. It has accommodation for thirty patients.

3. The Peiyang Women's Hospital, started five years ago in connection with the Woman's Medical School for the training of nurses. This contains twenty-two beds.

For a city like Tientsin, with over a million inhabitants, the hospital facilities are indeed small, and as a result thousands of sufferers pass yearly to an early grave, and no opportunity exists for the careful study of diseases and disease conditions in these parts.

Inasmuch as the climatic and other conditions in Tientsin differ considerably from other parts of China, we venture to describe briefly the Hospital we have in mind:

1. The hospital should be built in the Chinese city in close proximity to the Foreign Concessions, so as to be within easy reach of patients from both sides. The land could, if necessary, be asked from the Government, and the site chosen should possess ample room for extension and be close to the river or canal for drainage purposes.

2. It should have sufficient accommodation for 250 in-patients, and include wards for surgical, medical, gynecological and children's cases. A number of beds should be reserved for paying cases and for patients of other nationalities than Chinese. The main building should be a double-storied one, fitted up in the most modern way for the prosecution of research and teaching, particularly in surgical technique and sanitary science.

3. As there exist great extremes of heat and cold (varying from 115F or 46C in summer to 14F or -10C in winter) the hospital should be built to meet these requirements. The land in Tientsin is unusually flat, water being found less than four feet beneath the surface. Coal is abundant and cheap, and the hospital could with advantage supply its own electric lighting and steam heating.

4. The staff of the hospital should consist of a superintendent, one chief surgeon, one chief physician, one pharmacist (if possible, an analytical chemist, to study some of the more important drugs used by native physicians), and a head nurse—all Americans—together with a junior staff of Chinese assistant doctors, dressers, and nurses.

5. The hospital should be controlled by a board of trustees appointed by the donor. Until such a time as the trustees consider ripe for the self-support of the institution or its being passed over to Chinese management, the hospital should be built, maintained and controlled by the donor through the board of trustees.

We feel confident that such a hospital is urgently needed in China, and that it will not only benefit the sick and suffering, but also create a true and healthy spirit among Chinese of the aims and ideals of Western medical science in preventing as well as treating diseases.

We unanimously and earnestly request you to give the above your favorable consideration.

We have the honour to be, Sir,
Yours respectfully,

Name.	Occupation.	Address.
Robert Yü (W. R. U. & N. Y. State)	Physician and Surgeon	Tientsin.
S. C. Thomas Sze (Cornell)	Mechanical Engineer	"
Thomas A. Kuo (Harvard)	Lawyer	"
H. W. Ho (Yale)	Civil Engineer	"
P. N. Henry Sze (Syracuse)	Mechanical Engineer	"
Tsao Kuo Tsao (Cornell)		"
Tao Yüan Chen (Cornell)		"
Pond M. Jee (California)	Physician and Surgeon	"
Ju Hsiang Chen (California)		
Shang Him Yung (Polytechnic, Hartford)	Pg Mo Lin. Shipping Dptment. C. G. Ry.	"
Lew G. Kay (Washington)	Teacher	Tangshan.
C. S. Lin (Pennsylvania)	Financier	"
C. L. Yao		"
Y. T. Lou	Legal Adviser to Chihli Tutu.	"
S. M. Chung (Harvard)	Board of Education	"
C. T. Li (Harvard)	Teacher	"
T. C. Ma (Harvard)		"
C. Y. Tang		"
K. L. Wu (Cornell)	Electric Engineer	
Pien Yin Chang	President Chamber of Commerce	"
Liu Yun Shou	President of Tientsin District Assembly	"
Hu Yuan Hwei	President of Chihli Provincial Assembly	Ho-pei, Tientsin.
Wang Kuan Pao	President of Municipal Council	Tientsin.
Wu Lien Teh (M. A., M. D., Cantab.)	Assistant Director, Army Medical Coll., Med. Off. Foreign Off., Peking	"
Li Chin Tsao	Chief Secretary Provincial Educational Board (Chihli).	"

Name.	Occupation.	Address.
Wang Shoh Lian	President, Peiyang University.	
Sung Tse Chiu	Chairman of Delegates from all Provinces to Congress of Education, 1912	Tientsin.
Yen Chi Yi	Manager of Tung Ching Lung Firm (largest firm of silk merchants in Tientsin)	"
Hu Chia Chi	Proprietor of Tientsin Soap Factory	"
Chang Poling	President of Normal School	"
Yamei Kin	Principal of Nankai Middle School	"
H. Y. Kwan	Superintendent, Peiyang Woman's Medical School and Hospital	"
H. Y. King	Co-Director Peiyang Med. College	"
W. T. Watt	Professor, Peiyang Med. Coll. Superintendent of Studies of Coll.	"
Cheng Yik Kee	Director of Peiyang Medical College	"
	Director of Sanitary Board	"
	Compradore of Butterfield & Swire. Chairman of Cantonese Guild and Community	"

APPENDIX III

Memorial for the Endowment of a Free Public Library in Peking, China

To the Trustees of the
  Carnegie Endowment for International Peace:

SIRS:
   We, the undersigned, all of whom are or have lately been concerned with education in China, have the honor to present to the Trustees of the Carnegie Endowment for International Peace the following memorial:—

   The revolution in China is a movement to substitute for a despotic government, under which neither life nor property was secure, especially in the official and higher commercial classes, a government under just and equal laws, enacted by representatives of that portion of the people which has received some measure of education, and binding alike on rulers and ruled, rich and poor, educated and illiterate.

   For ultimate success in establishing a strong, unified, and stable national government, under which the right to "life, liberty, and the pursuit of happiness" will be secured to the whole population, the republican movement must rely on the gradual diffusion, among the Chinese people, of education and of Western ideals of order and liberty under law.

   We believe that the safe progress of good government in China might be effectively promoted, year after year, by a free public library conducted in Peking under the American plan; and we therefore unanimously and earnestly request the Trustees to establish and maintain such a library under their own direction for the present, but with the ultimate intention of transferring it in due time to the Chinese Central Government or to a board of trustees resident in China.

   In as much as the library might well have some functions not commonly exercised by American public libraries, we venture to describe briefly the institution we have in mind:

   1. It should be placed in Peking, the capital city, where many office-holders and candidates for office will always be living, where several important educational institutions already exist, and more are likely to be created, and where the legations and the headquarters of the press correspondents are established.

   2. For Peking it should maintain a free reading room, open day and evening, and a good collection of reference books on such subjects as agriculture, mining, the fundamental trades, economics, geography, commerce, sanitation, public works, government, public administration, international law, and the judicial settlement of disputes between nations.

   3. It should also permit any book, which has been in the library one year, and does not belong to the reference collection, to be borrowed for home use, during a period not exceeding twenty days, provided the borrower, if living outside of Peking, pay the postage.

   4. It should also, through a special officer, select, translate, edit and circulate leaflets and booklets containing useful information on any or all of the subjects above mentioned (cf. 2), the distribution being made gratuitously, first to Chinese newspapers and periodicals, secondly to educational institutions, thirdly, to appropriate government officials, and fourthly, to private persons on request.

MEMORIAL FOR A FREE PUBLIC LIBRARY IN PEKING.

We feel confident that such an institution would gradually acquire great influence in China, and hence in the whole Orient; and that it would effectively promote good government, industrial and commercial prosperity, and thus, the peace of the world.

We have the honor to be, Sirs,

Yours respectfully,

Name.	Occupation.	Address.
V. K. Wellington Koo (Columbia)	Secretary of the Cabinet	The Known Yuan, Peking.
Tsang Kwong-Sheung (Penna.)	Private Secretary to Premier	The Known Yuan, Peking.
Y. C. Lung (Pennsylvania)	Private Secretary to President Yüan	Office of the President, Peking.
Jen H. Jee (Harvard)	Private Secretary to President Yüan	Office of the President, Peking.
Ts'ai Ting Kan (Hartford High School)	Naval Secretary to the President	Office of the President, Peking.
Hugh G. H. Tong (Harvard)	Forest Inspector to Manchuria	Board of Agriculture.
Victor L. Young (Albany Business College)		Returned Students Club.
Ching Chun Wong (Yale and University of Illinois)	Ministry of Communications	Peking University, Peking.
Liang Lai Kwei (Massachusetts Agricultural College and Cornell University)	Head of the Agricultural Station	Peking University.
Li Chien Luan (Columbia)		Tientsin.
L. C. Chu (Yale)		Peking.
K. L. Carlos Sun (Cornell)	Board of Communications	Peking.
N. T. Woo (California and Wisconsin)	Director, College of Commerce, Peking University	Peking.
T. E. Ing (Pennsylvania)		Peking.
Witson S. Shan (Columbia)		Peking.
Lo Chong (Oxford)	Board of Communications	Peking.
T. C. Sun (Cornell)	Director of Kirin Changchung Railway	Changchun, Manchuria.
Mun-Yen Chung (Yale, '83)		Shanghai.
P. A. C. Tzan	Honorable Secretary North-China American College Club, English Secretary to the President	Waichiao Pu, Peking.
Yu Chuan Chang	Attaché to the Foreign Office, ex-Hon. Treasurer North-China American College Club	Waichiao Pu, Peking.
Koliang Yit	Dean of College of Agriculture and Director of Experiment Station	Government University, Peking.
W. L. Chun (West Point)	Captain, General Staff	General Staff (3rd Bureau), Peking.
W. C. Chen	Editor of the Peking Daily News	Peking Daily News, Peking.
Luther M. Jee (California)	Professor of Political Economy, College of Finance, Peking	c/o Peking Daily News Office, Peking.

MEMORIAL FOR A FREE PUBLIC LIBRARY IN PEKING.

Name.	Occupation.	Address.
P. H. Linn	Editor of the Peking Daily News	c/o Peking Daily News Office, Peking.
Chao S. Bok	Senator for Kwang-tung	Peking.
H. B. Kingman (Philadelphia)	Dental Surgeon	23 Rue du Baron Gros, Tientsin.
		Morrison St., Peking.
Wu Kuei Ling (Cornell)	Electrical Engineer	Peking-Mukden Line.
Tsok Kai Tse (Massachusetts Institute of Technology)	Mining Engineer	Peking.
Julian Kwan (Yale)	C. G. Railways	Tientsin.
Yen TeChing (Lehigh)	Ministry of Posts and Communications	Peking.

We, the undersigned, comprising Chinese who have at one time or another been educated in America, desire to express our hearty support and cordial approval of the Memorial to the Trustees of the Carnegie Endowment for International Peace for the establishment of a free public library in Peking.

TONG SHAO YI (*Premier*).
(Columbia.)
CHENGTING T. WANG (*Acting Minister Industry and Commerce*).
(Yale.)
WANG CHUNG HUI (*Minister of Justice*).
(Yale.)

SUPPLEMENTARY LIST OF SIGNERS TO THE LIBRARY MEMORIAL.

Sao-Ke Alfred Sze	Secretary of Communications	Peking.
W. W. Yen	Second Secretary of Foreign Affairs	"
Yen Fuh	President Government University	"
Tsai Yuen Beh	Secretary of Education	"
Fan Yuan Lin	Second Secretary of Education	"
George Ernest Morrison, M.D.	Correspondent of the *London Times*	"
S. Sung Young	President Tongshan Engineering College	
Tong Kaison	President Chinghua College	
P. K. C. Tyau	Interpreter and Secretary to President Yuan Shih Kai	"
J. B. Taylor	Principal of Anglo-Chinese College	Tientsin.
Wang Shoh Lian	President Pei-yang University	"
Yen Shiu	Former Vice-Minister of Education	Peking.
Yamei Kin, M.D.	Superintendent Pei-yang Woman's Medical School and Hospital	Tientsin.
Gilbert Reid, D.D.	President International Institute of China	Shanghai.
Chang-Po-Ling	Principal of Nankai Middle School	Tientsin.
Wu Lien-Teh, M.D.	Deputy-Director Army Medical College and Medical Adviser to the Foreign Office	Tientsin.
Chu Chi	Editor of the *Peking Daily News*	Peking.
Chang Yu-Shu	Honorary President General Chamber of Commerce	Peking.
Kang Shih-To	Editor of the Chinese Daily, *Minsupao*	Peking.
Charles D. Tenney, LL.D.	Former President Pei-yang University and Adviser on Education to the Imperial Government	Tientsin.
Sung Chi-Chiu	Merchant	Tientsin.

APPENDIX IV
Letter of Dr. Charles W. Eliot to Hon. Tong Shao-yi

TIENTSIN, N. CHINA, *May 1, 1912.*

HON. TONG SHAO-YI,
    Peking.
MY DEAR SIR:

In the conversation which I lately had the honor of holding with you, I endeavored to describe as briefly as possible the measures which seem indispensable to success in procuring soon for the government of China proper credit in the money-lending markets of the world. I was not thinking of the immediate measures necessary for obtaining the loan of a sum of money sufficient to carry on the government for a year or eighteen months, but of those durable and far-reaching measures that would give the government a sure and ample income for decades and generations to come. To procure such an income, and hence the financial credit which is necessary to the independence and honor of China, I ventured to state that two measures were essential: (1) The Central Government must obtain, by methods of taxation that have approved themselves to Western economists and statesmen, an annual income sufficient for the present needs of the republic, and likely to increase with the increasing prosperity of the country. (2) This income must be expended honestly and effectively on objects and in methods which have proved good in Western administrations.

To secure these two all-important ends, it is obvious that in the actual condition of the Chinese civil and military service, foreign advisers must be procured and given enough authority to convince Western capitalists and governments that an adequate national income is going to be secured, and that it is to be spent in a modern, scientific way. When I had the privilege of talking with you at Shanghai and at Peking, I understood you to think that foreign advisers were indispensable to the new Republican Government in the actual crisis, and should be employed by the government itself for specific terms of years, without nomination by any foreign government or combination of governments. I beg to say that I agree very heartily with these views of yours. While I believe that many foreign experts should be employed with the utmost possible promptness, I also believe that it would be unwise for the government of China to accept such experts on the nomination of officials or representatives of the Great Powers. I have also been given to understand that the present Chinese government would find it very difficult to select competent and trustworthy foreign advisers, partly from lack of knowledge, and partly from lack of practice in judging the character and ability of individual foreigners.

As you know, I have already given to Colonel Tsai Ting Kan, the interpreter to the President, the suggestion that the Trustees of the Carnegie Endowment for International Peace would be a very suitable body to nominate to the Chinese Government men selected from several Western nationalities (especially the smaller ones) who would be competent advisers in the several departments of the Republican Government needing such assistance.

At the conversation I had with the President on Friday last, through your good offices, it seemed to me that he had not been put in possession of my suggestion, and, because of your silence, I was not sure that you fully apprehended the arguments I stated to the interpreter. I beg leave, therefore, to put before you in writing a description of the Carnegie Endowment for International Peace and of its Trustees.

In the first place, the Endowment has a permanent body of Trustees, filling their own vacancies, possessed of a liberal income (£100,000 sterling a year), intended to be perpetual, likely to endure for centuries, having for its main object the promotion of International Peace, but also proposing to promote those agencies and sentiments which make towards peace, such as education, religious toleration, public order, the coöperation of capital and labor in industries, equal laws, public justice, a permanent international tribunal, and all institutions which can cultivate good will among men. The Trustees receive no salaries or other emoluments. Their efforts must necessarily be of an international sort. They must be impartial, independent, and disinterested; and their work must be laid out not for tomorrow, or for next year, but on far-reaching plans. The Trustees deal now with scholars, men of affairs, and statesmen in all the leading nations, and are acquainted with leading experts on all subjects in the principal Western nations. The Trustees are men of experience in educational, industrial, or governmental affairs; in support of this statement I need only cite the names of a few of the Trustees:

Elihu Root. Former Secretary of State. Now a Senator in Congress from the State of New York.
Joseph H. Choate. Former Ambassador at the Court of St. James, and one of the representatives of the United States at the Second Hague Conference.
Charlemagne Tower. Former Ambassador at Berlin.
Oscar S. Straus. Former Ambassador at Constantinople, and Secretary for Commerce and Labor in President Roosevelt's Cabinet.
Henry S. Pritchett. Formerly Superintendent of the United States Coast Survey; then President of the Massachusetts Institute of Technology; now President of the Carnegie Foundation for the Advancement of Teaching.
Robert S. Woodward. President of the Carnegie Institution for Promoting Scientific Research.
Nicholas Murray Butler. President of Columbia University, New York.

The gentlemen named above who have served as representatives of the American government in foreign countries are now simply private citizens. The Trustees of the Carnegie Endowment for International Peace are as impartial a body of men as can be imagined, and are recognized as such among all the Western nations; they are also competent as judges of men. Finally, they are all actuated by the friendliest sentiments towards China.

My suggestion was that the nominations made by the Trustees of the Carnegie Endowment should be subject to the veto of some representative of the Chinese government residing in Washington, either the Chinese Minister, or some person especially appointed for this work by the Chinese government.

I did not intend that this method of selecting foreign advisers should preclude the Government of China from selecting a few principal advisers quite of their own motion—such as the general advisers for the President, for the Prime Minister, and for the Secretary for Foreign Affairs,—whenever the government could take such action with full knowledge of the true quality of the men selected; but I understood during my recent visit to Peking, that the present government has full knowledge of very few men competent to serve as foreign advisers. Indeed I heard the name of only one person whom Chinese and foreigners would alike regard as competent and altogether desirable as adviser to the President and his Cabinet. That name was William W. Rockhill.

From the conversations I have had with leading men in Peking, both Chinese and foreigners, during the ten days past (April 19 to 29), I feel a strong conviction that if the President and Cabinet should now make two announcements without consulting any foreign government or minister, as follows: (1) We propose to invite William W. Rockhill to the service of the Chinese government as General Adviser, and (2) We propose to ask the Carnegie Endowment for International Peace to select the numerous foreign experts whom the Chinese government is conscious that it needs, the position of the Republic in regard to its capacity to borrow money and also in regard to recognition by foreign powers would immediately be much strengthened.

I expect to be in Tientsin for two weeks to come; and if at any time within this limit you desire to talk further with me concerning any of the measures herein proposed, I shall hold myself at your disposition in Peking.

I beg leave to add that I have not consulted the American Minister, or any other foreign official, about the proposals made in this letter. They proceed from an American private citizen experienced in educational administration and one of the Trustees of the Carnegie Endowment, namely, myself.

I am, with high regard,

Sincerely yours,
(Signed) CHARLES W. ELIOT.

APPENDIX V

An International Hospital for Tokyo
MEMORIAL TO THE TRUSTEES OF THE CARNEGIE ENDOWMENT.

GENTLEMEN:

President Eliot has consented to present this Memorial and bring before you the situation here in Tokyo in regard to the development of the present St. Luke's Hospital into an International Peace Institution.

The standing of the hospital in the community and the requirements of the situation offer unique opportunities for establishing a work which will exert in a most practical way far-reaching influence for International Peace. No more fitting monument to international good will and mutual understanding could well be established in Tokyo than an International Hospital conducted along the lines now pursued by St. Luke's Hospital, with its active and consulting staff of Japanese and foreign physicians and surgeons, a Nurses' Training School, under foreign and Japanese direction, and a successful Medical Society with both Japanese and foreigners as active and honorary members.

The position gained by St. Luke's Hospital during the past ten years in the confidence of both the Japanese and foreign public in Japan would insure the success of such an undertaking and the logical development of present conditions. Such an institution would at once be a practical working example of good will, mutual help, and sympathy between foreigners of all nations and Japanese, and a very positive and constant influence for better understanding and closer friendship.

As the hospital accommodation for the care of foreigners in Tokyo and throughout Japan is very little understood by those who have not lived in the Empire and had experiences of conditions, some explanation is necessary for a clear understanding of the situation.

Tokyo has a number of highly qualified and efficient native physicians and surgeons, and a small group of brilliant laboratory and scientific medical investigators who compare favorably with the best in America and Europe. Also Tokyo has a few large and efficient hospitals for the care of the Japanese, besides a very large number of small private institutions. But there is no arrangement made anywhere in Japanese hospitals for the medical or surgical care of foreigners. Also there is no provision whereby the foreigner may have easy and certain access to the best that Tokyo has to offer in its medical, surgical and laboratory specialists.

This is the situation so far as the foreigner is concerned and for the past ten years it has been the effort of St. Luke's Hospital to fill the very obvious gap and provide a thoroughly modern hospital under foreign management where the nursing, diet, heating, sanitary arrangements, and control of the patients are best suited for the care of foreigners, and where they may at once secure the services of the best specialist in the city if necessary, according to the requirements of each case. The real need for such an institution is well attested by the signal success with which St. Luke's has met, and the positive approval and endorsement of the institution and its aims by practically the whole of the foreign and Japanese community in Japan and the leading members of the Japanese medical profession in Tokyo. For the benefit of those not intimately familiar with the situation here it is well to explain why foreigners are neither acceptable nor comfortable in Japanese hospitals:

1. Japanese hospitals make no arrangements at all for the care of foreigners, and their presence in the hospital is a very disturbing problem. The barrier of the language makes it almost impossible for the assistant doctors and the nurses to take proper care of foreigners. The effort of an ill foreigner to make himself understood and the confusion and misunderstandings arising therefrom have more than once worked serious harm and even fatally prejudiced recovery.

2. There are, of course, no provisions made in a Japanese hospital for foreign diet and the many conveniences required by foreigners when ill. The dieting and post-operative care of patients, as all physicians know, is of the greatest importance and influence in the ultimate termination of each case.

3. There is a third and very important reason why foreigners are a disturbing and perplexing element in Japanese hospitals, and often suffer serious harm when everything is being attempted for their comfort and welfare by the hospital authorities. We refer to the difficulty repeatedly experienced by the Japanese of properly controlling foreign patients. Much of this lack of control is due to the fact that Japanese hospitals are not prepared to take in foreigners and are inexperienced in managing them. One foreign patient and his relatives and friends will often give more trouble in a Japanese hospital than a dozen or more equally ill Japanese patients. This soon leads to confusion and bad management of the case, and frequently serious consequences are the result. It is a fact that Japanese physicians of eminence have repeatedly refused to assume the responsibility of treating foreign patients in Japanese hospitals because, in part at least, of the risk to their reputations entailed by the inadequate management and care the case would have to receive.

4. The heating, sanitary arrangements and general regime in a Japanese hospital are not satisfactory for the care of a foreigner.

The Japanese fully realize all of these conditions and are themselves opposed to admitting foreign patients into their hospitals because of these difficulties and their general lack of preparation.

Tokyo is the logical and proper place for the establishment of an International Hospital in the Far East. The fact that the city affords the best medical, surgical and laboratory specialists in the Far East is of paramount importance. The climate is excellent and the city affords modern conveniences and a good market.

Tokyo is really the gateway to the Far East and within easy reach of the ports of China, Korea and Manchuria. St. Luke's Hospital now draws patients from places as far distant as Singapore, Java, Hongkong, Vladivostock, and the East Manchurian cities, besides the more numerous cases from Japan proper and Korea.

The number of embassies and legations in Tokyo, in addition to the large and increasing number of foreign residents, visitors and tourists, makes the city especially appropriate for the establishment of an International Hospital.

With a well-equipped hospital under foreign management patients from the tropics, from the coast and inland cities of China, the Philippines and Manchuria, could come to Tokyo with its superior climate, sure of receiving proper hospital care, and the skill and treatment of the best Japanese specialists if necessary.

The mountain resorts of Japan offer excellent accommodations for the care of convalescents, and they are within easy reach of Tokyo.

It is material to the subject to view this question of an International Hospital in Tokyo from the standpoint of the Japanese for their own use.

The hospitals in Tokyo can be divided into two classes:

I. Those hospitals conducted by the government for government purposes: The Red Cross, the official hospital of the Red Cross Society, open in part to the public in time of peace; the Army and Navy Hospitals, exclusively for those branches of the service; and the University Hospital, conducted to furnish clinical material for the university students. (It seems advisable to point out here that in Japan a hospital run for the purpose of furnishing clinical material is conducted on the most economical lines and is only of service to absolute charity cases. The situation is entirely different in America.)

II. Private hospitals carried on by one or more doctors for their own personal benefit.

Also the Mitsui Charity Hospital, built and maintained through the generosity of the Mitsui family, should be mentioned. This hospital has 150 beds strictly for charity cases, and its great success points very clearly to the need for several more such institutions for the assistance of the large number of poor and needy in Tokyo.

None of these hospitals, however, are conducted as are general hospitals in America where a patient may call in consultation any reputable physician, or specialist, as the case may demand. The Japanese public, especially the educated classes, feel the lack of such an institution clearly, and an International Hospital fulfilling this need would at once be sure of their sympathy and support.

The Japanese would, of course, welcome a hospital providing 50 charity beds for the city and a large free dispensary giving treatment to 100 or more charity cases a day.

The plan for the International Hospital would be a development of the present work already well under way in St. Luke's. The hospital should be situated on a fairly large piece of land with sufficient grounds surrounding it for the use of the patients.

Total accommodation for at least 150 beds should be provided. The hospital would include a central administration building; a building for pay cases, Japanese and foreign, to contain about 100 beds; and a charity department, containing some 50 beds exclusively for charity patients, either Japanese or foreign. Attached to this charity department should be a large free dispensary open daily to the public.

The hospital buildings should be reinforced concrete, or some other fire-proof material, and the equipment, of course, thoroughly modern in every way.

The central administration building should contain consulting rooms and a lecture and assembly hall for the use of the Medical Society attached to the hospital.

A suitable building should be erected for a nurses' home and ample facilities provided for a thoroughly modern school for nurses. Quarters for the staff and students could be included in the administration building, or provided for separately. A separate ward for insane cases would be a necessity, as at present there is no provision at all anywhere in Japan for the care of foreign insane cases. Repeatedly this lack has been a great hardship and of serious consequences to foreign patients. The government refuses any responsibility in the matter; and provision even of the most modest type would often prove of the greatest practical use. Cases of temporary insanity, or drug addiction, are fairly frequently met with here in the East, and they always prove a very perplexing problem.

A special department for hydro-therapeutic treatment and the care of patients suffering from neurasthenia should be included. Cases of neurasthenia are very common in the East amongst foreigners, and the necessity of sending them home for treatment means heavy expense, and, on this account, frequently serious delay in applying proper treatment. There is no reason at all why patients suffering with neurasthenia should not have entirely satisfactory treatment in Japan if proper hospital facilities and equipments are provided. A hospital equipped with modern hydro-therapeutic apparatus in so central a place as Tokyo would be of the greatest economic value for the treatment of patients from China and throughout the Far East.

Besides the provision for surgical, medical and children's wards, arrangement should be made for the treatment of eye, ear and throat cases.

The regular attending staff of the hospital should contain at least three foreign and about six Japanese physicians and surgeons. The Japanese staff would be selected from the University of Tokyo graduates. The consulting staff of the hospital would consist of the professors of the Tokyo Imperial University in their several specialties and a number of the leading members of the medical profession in Tokyo. The Imperial Government Laboratory, under the direction of Professor Kitazato, would continue its present connection with St. Luke's as consulting laboratory.

The hospital house staff should consist of about eight young medical graduates who would serve for a period of three years for the benefit of obtaining postgraduate hospital experience.

The arrangement outlined above is similar to the plan now in operation in St. Luke's on a smaller scale, and it has been found very satisfactory.

About a year ago a medical society was founded in connection with St. Luke's Hospital. This promises to be a marked addition to the resources of the work, and the practical interest taken by the members is very encouraging. It is the only medical society under foreign management in Japan and at present its sympathies are largely American.

The fact that the professors of the Medical Department of the Tokyo Imperial University are willing to act as consultants for St. Luke's is a very high tribute to the institution, and it is of the greatest importance in planning for the International Hospital.

The education of Japanese seeking admission to the medical department of the University is entirely in German and along German lines; and the influence subsequent to his graduation is German, so far as his professional studies are concerned. The foreign text books are exclusively German. Hundreds of medical graduates go to Germany for postgraduate work. Practically none go to America, though many speak English. This, however good, is very one-sided and something should be done in a practical and definite way to turn the attention of the medical profession here in Japan to America, and have at least a part of their students go there for postgraduate schooling. A successful International Hospital and Medical Society with strong American interest and backing would go far to correct this rather one-sided development of medicine in Japan.

With the exchange of students and college men, and their association together, better understanding and appreciation of one another is developed and through such men the cause of international peace is much advanced.

The accommodation of the present St. Luke's, including the new rooms built this summer, is about 75 beds. Of these about 30 are for charity patients.

The need in Japan for a hospital as outlined in this Memorial is very real and pressing. Hardly an educated Japanese or foreigner can be found who will dispute this statement. As a practical illustration of friendship and international good will and a strong influence for international peace its usefulness would be very great indeed. The truth of this statement becomes quite apparent if local conditions and the character of the Japanese people are studied.

For many years the establishment and support of medical work by missionary boards has been a well recognized and very successful method of introducing Christianity; and many are of the opinion that on the whole this is the most successful and practical way of reaching the people of a foreign land and winning their confidence and coöperation. If medical work and hospitals are such a success in mission fields why would not similar methods be of equal advantage in spreading the doctrine of international peace? Would not the establishment of such a hospital be a direct step in bringing home to the people the teachings of international peace? Only by establishing between nations a strong public opinion of mutual understanding and sympathy can misconceptions be cleared away and a true foundation for international peace be laid. The Japanese are peculiarly responsive to any definite overtures directed towards a practical solution of their immediate needs. The good will and deeper desire for friendly relations prompting such an offer of assistance would be keenly appreciated and very highly valued. As a people they are especially sensitive to friendly advances, and the depth and extent of public sentiment aroused by an act of this kind can hardly be realized by one who has not lived amongst them. A hospital built in Tokyo in the interest of international peace, largely through the generosity of Americans, would at once be known and discussed throughout the Empire. Would it not appeal in a more definite and tangible way to a much larger audience than do many of the methods usually adopted in the spreading of the ideals of international peace?

In this connection it should be remembered that with the establishment of the hospital its influence in moulding public opinion has just begun. The admission of each case would being vividly before the minds of those interested in the patient the cause for which the institution was erected. The good effect of this upon the minds of the Japanese is much more positive and far reaching than would be the case in Occidental lands.

A powerful potential aid in extending the sphere of influence of the hospital has recently been embodied in a request received from several prominent Japanese connected with the Department of Communications, that a training school for nurses be organized in connection with St. Luke's and especially that the training be Christian. The nurses would receive, in addition to their regular training, special instruction along Christian lines and every influence brought to bear that this teaching make a strong impress upon their lives and work. A corps of district nurses would be trained, and as soon as possible stations throughout Tokyo would be established. The school would also provide twice a year special courses in practical instruction for young women in home nursing and the care of children. This is a very practical plan and it fits the needs in Tokyo closely. At present the position of a Japanese trained nurse is little, if any, better than an ordinary servant. The great majority of them have only a few months theoretical training before entering on their life's work, and no effort is made at all from a moral standpoint to protect them in the discharge of their duties. The custom in Japanese hospitals of the nurses sleeping in the room with their patients is very pernicious and highly objectionable. This custom alone keeps the standing of nurses in Japan much lower than it would otherwise be. It is essential that women of a better class apply for training before the standard of nursing can be materially raised. Christian teaching and protection will go far to guarantee this. Present conditions are largely the result of false standards and limited training. In almost all countries the trained nurse is more or less under religious instruction and protection, and often she is a direct development of a group of nursing sisters or other religious body. In Japan this is not true. Nursing is merely a means of earning a living and there is no religious, ethical, or humanitarian viewpoint connected with it. A well organized Christian school for training nurses along American lines, and a system of district nursing introduced into Tokyo would revolutionize present conditions and do untold good for the Japanese people. Such a school connected with a hospital openly conducted in the interest of international peace would greatly widen its influence and emphasize the ideals for which it stands.

To put this plan for an International Hospital in Tokyo into successful operation about $500,000 would be necessary. Of this amount $200,000 would be required for purchasing a suitable site and the remaining $300,000 would be needed for buildings and equipment.

Should the Trustees appropriate sufficient funds for the building, the money necessary for the purchase of the land would undoubtedly be raised in Japan and through the friends of St. Luke's Hospital.

A grant from the Carnegie Peace Fund could be made conditional upon the raising of this money for the land.

It has been clearly ascertained that a self-perpetuating board of trustees can be formed under Japanese law to constitute a juridical person for the purpose of holding title to all properties, either real or personal, pertaining to the hospital.

AN INTERNATIONAL HOSPITAL FOR TOKYO.

The plan for an International Hospital in Tokyo has been under discussion and serious consideration for several years and the endorsers of this Memorial have had ample opportunity to investigate the question and fully inform themselves of the real conditions present. Since the inception of the plan several years ago Sir Claude MacDonald, the British Ambassador to Tokyo, has given it his enthusiastic support and never allowed an opportunity to pass without doing all in his power to further it. Sir Claude's long residence in the East and his intimate knowledge of Japan and the Japanese give peculiar weight to his endorsement and especially qualifies him to speak with authority in this matter.

In closing, it is considered by the writers only fair to state that the gentlemen signing this Memorial have been carefully selected because they are amongst the leading men, native and foreign, in Japan today, and most widely represent the best thought for the welfare of the country and the cause of international peace.

Respectfully yours,

Charles Page Bryan,
  American Ambassador.
Marquis Guiccioli,
  Italian Ambassador.
N. Maluosky Maluvitch,
  Russian Ambassador.
Charles Campbell, Jr.,
  Second Secretary of the American Embassy to Japan.
Claude M. MacDonald,
  British Ambassador.
A. Gérard,
  Ambassadeur de France.
Baron G. Franckenstein,
  Austro-Hungarian Chargé d'Affaires.
Yeiji Asabuki.
John McKim,
  Bishop of Tokyo.
Cecil,
  Bishop of the English Missions in South Tokyo.
J. Russell Kennedy,
  The Associated Press.
Prof. Dr. S. Goto.
K. Doli,
  Prof. of Dermatology, Tokyo Imperial University.
Prof. Dr. T. Hirota,
  University of Tokyo.
T. Aoyama,
  Dean of the Medical Faculty, University of Tokyo.
Dr. W. Okada,
  Prof., College of Medicine, University of Tokyo.
Dr. Komoto,
  Prof., College of Medicine, University of Tokyo.
Dr. S. Kinoshita,
  Director of Department of Gynecology, University of Tokyo.
Lorenzo N. Rider,
  Director of Nippon Electric Co., Ltd., Tokyo.
Count Shigenobu Okuma.
Rev. Clay MacCauley.
Henry T. Terry,
  Prof., Imperial University.
Rev. Daniel Crosby Greene, D.D.
D. Browning,
  British Naval Attaché.
A. W. Medley,
  Instructor, Imperial University.
Thomas F. Nonweiler,
  Asst. Mgr., Tokyo Marine Insurance Co.
Mark Napier Trollope,
  Bishop in Korea.
Walter Andrews,
  Bishop of Yokohama.
Hugh James Foss,
  Bishop in Osaka.
Thomas Bliss, M.D.,
  Physician, St. Luke's Hospital.
R. B. Teusler, M.D.,
  Director, St. Luke's Hospital.
F. Brinkley,
  Editor in Chief, *Japan Mail*.
J. T. Shipp,
  Prof. of English Literature, Tokyo Imperial University and Higher Normal School.
Louis Bridel, Prof., Imperial University, Tokyo.
I. N. Penlington,
  Proprietor of the *Far East*.
John Struthers,
  Chilian Nitrate Propaganda for Japan, China, and the Far East.
H. St. George Tucker,
  Bishop of Kyoto.
Viscount Aoki,
  Former Ambassador to the United States of America.
F. C. Sale,
  For Sale & Frazer, Ltd.
Charles J. Arnell,
  Japanese Secretary, American Embassy, Tokyo.

Baron D. Kikuchi, M.P. (Cambridge, M.A.), President Imperial University, Kyoto; ex-President Peers' School; ex-Minister Education, etc.
H. E. Marquis Terauchi, Governor-General of Korea; ex-Minister War; Chief of the General Staff, etc.
Baron Yeiichi Shibusawa, Founder First Bank of Japan (Das Ichi Ginke); Chairman Chamber of Commerce; Director of several of the largest business enterprises in Japan.
Baron C. Kikkawa, Member House of Peers, etc.
Baron K. Ishii, Vice-Minister Foreign Affairs; Minister to Rome, etc.
Baron H. Sakatani, ex-Minister Finance, etc.
Y. Ozaki, Esq., M. P., Mayor of Tokyo; ex-Minister of Education, etc.
Viscount Y. Hanabusa, ex-Minister Imperial Household; Vice-President Japan Red Cross Society; Minister of Agriculture, etc.
Baron Naibu Kanda, Member of the House of Peers; Professor Imperial University, Tokyo.
Viscount K. Kaneko, Privy Councillor and President America's Friend Society.
A. Kabayama, Esq., Director Hakodate Dockyard Co.
T. Kadono, Esq., Nihon Commercial Co.
Y. Komora, Esq., Director Mitsui Busen Kaisha.
S. Asano, Esq., President and Director Toyo Kisen Kaisha (Oriental Steamship Company).
T. Miyaoka, Esq.
M. Zumoto, Esq., Proprietor and Editor *Japan Times*.
Y. Asabuki, Esq.
Dr. Asakura, Director Asakura Hospital.
Professor Kuodo,
Professor Sato,
Professor Miura,
Professor Tashiro, } Medical Department, Imperial University, Tokyo.
Professor Komoto,
Professor Hamao,
Professor Irisama,
Professor Kizazato, Head of the Imperial Government Bureau of Sanitation and Director of the Government Pathological Laboratories and Institute.
Professor Shiga, Imperial Government Laboratory, Tokyo.
Dr. Hata, Imperial Government Laboratory, Tokyo.
Professor Kitajima, Imperial Government Institute, Tokyo.
Professor Shibayama, Imperial Government Institute, Tokyo.
Professor Miyajima, Imperial Government Institute, Tokyo.
Hon. H. W. Denison, Adviser Foreign Office, Tokyo.
Baron Von Radowitz, First Secretary, German Embassy, Tokyo.
Mr. Thomas Sammons, American Consul-General, Yokohama.
Mr. William T. Payne, Director for the East Canadian Pacific Railway Co.
Mr. R. J. Kirby.
Mr. P. K. Condict, Nippon Electric Co.
Mr. E. Q. Frazer, Sale & Frazer, Tokyo.
Mr. H. C. Goold, Standard Oil Co., Yokohama.
Mr. B. W. Fleisher, Editor, *Japan Advertiser*.
Rev. H. Loomis.
Mr. H. W. Andrews, Andrews & George, Tokyo.
Mr. E. W. George, Andrews & George, Tokyo.
Mr. Henry B. Metcalf, Babcock & Wilcox, Ltd., Tokyo.
Mr. David Thompson.
Mr. E. R. Pallister, Nippon Yusen Kaisha.
Mr. W. E. Strong.
Mr. F. L. Booth.
Mr. E. D. Wolff, Siemens & Schuckert.
Mr. G. Lohe.
Mr. F. Wilhelm.
Mr. S. Sanderson.
Mr. H. N. Landis.
Dr. William Imbrie.
Dr. A. Oltmann.
Dr. E. R. Miller.

Dr. M. N. Wyckoff.
Rev. J. G. Ballagh.
L'Abbé M. Streichen.
L'Abbé H. Demangelle.
L'Abbé Beuve.
Mr. Montgomery Schuyler, First Secretary, American Embassy.
Mr. G. O. Wallenberg, Sweden Envoy Extraordinary and Minister Plenipotentiary.
Professor K. Aylmer Coates.
Rev. W. P. Buncombe.
Dr. J. N. Seymour.
Mr. W. H. Stone.
Mr. A. Schurbatsky, First Secretary, Russian Embassy.
Mr. J. H. von Royan, Netherlands Minister.
Mr. R. G. Pacheco, Mexican Minister.
Mr. H. M. G. Rumbold, Councillor and Chargé d'Affaires, British Embassy
Mr. D. M. Crackenthorpe, First Secretary, British Embassy.
Mr. S. M. Hobart-Hampden, Japanese Secretary, British Embassy.
Rev. L. Cholomondeley.
Count von Montgelas, German Embassy, Councillor.
Dr. Fuehr, Second Secretary, German Embassy.
Captain F. S. G. Piggott, Attaché, British Embassy.
Lt.-Col. J. A. C. Somerville, Military Attaché, British Embassy.

APPENDIX VI

Abstract of a Memorandum on the Subject of the Education of the Children of Foreigners Resident in the Far East—The Great Need of a Good Preparatory School

This Memorial is presented by kind permission, through Dr. Charles W. Eliot, President *Emeritus* of Harvard University.

Facilities offered in the Far East for the education of the children of foreigners are lamentably small. Foreigners living in the Philippines, China, Korea, Formosa, and Japan are obliged to send their children to Europe or America in order that they may attend good secondary schools.

Diplomats, educators, business men, missionaries, publicists, and all other foreign residents of the Far East who have considered the matter recognize the need of a first-class secondary school; and a Special Committee appointed in 1909 to investigate the subject decided upon Tokyo as the best site for the proposed school. Former efforts to establish a school of the kind desired have failed because of lack of endowment. The Tokyo School for Foreign Children provides for sixty day pupils of from nine to fifteen years of age, and the general facilities of the school have been brought to a reasonably good standard on a fair foundation; but this and other schools in Yokohama and Kobe are quite inadequate to provide educational facilities for even a small proportion of the American and European children who are ready to enter a secondary school as day or boarding-pupils.

The fact that families must be widely separated when the children are sent to European or American secondary schools may deter heads of households from accepting governmental or commercial positions in the Far East; or if the positions be accepted, it entails the sending of children at a critical age thousands of miles from home, with the resulting strain upon the affections and resources of the family. If a good secondary school were established convenient of access from many points, it is believed that it would prolong the residence in the Far East of parents engaged in governmental, commercial, or educational service, create better social, commercial, and governmental relations because of the increased opportunity for mutual acquaintance of Orientals and Occidentals, and thereby serve the cause of international peace.

Tokyo was chosen as the site of the proposed school, because of its favorable climate, transportation facilities, markets, excellent sanitation, and its social and intellectual advantages as the capital of Japan. In the suburbs of the city, easily reached by a street car service, are magnificent hillside sites for such a school, overlooking the sea.

The school should be endowed, and should be under Occidental directorship of the best type. If a consulting board of governors or an advisory council proved necessary, the members of such a board could be chosen from the diplomatic and consular services, and the professional, technical, and business classes in Tokyo.

The Special Committee has now brought the Tokyo Grammar School to the highest point of usefulness possible without an endowment. It has also begun to secure a guaranteed annual income of not less than yen 10,000 over and above the present income, and is considering plans for suitable buildings which would cost yen 200,000, or $100,000 gold. There is reason to hope that an adequate site for the school may be given by the Government or by leading Japanese banks and business houses, if it should seem wise to accept such a gift. An endowment of yen 500,000 to yen 750,000, $250,000 to $375,000 gold, would probably be necessary to the proper administration of the school.

It has been decided by the Committee that it would be well to open the school to Japanese day pupils who expect to finish their education in America or in England, and to include in the curriculum courses in Japanese conversation and Chinese character, for the benefit of American youth destined to commercial careers in the Orient.

Investigation has shown that such a school would be heartily welcomed and encouraged by the Japanese people; and the Presidents of Waseda, The Imperial, and Keio Universities have positively assured the writer of this memorial that these institutions will offer inducements to foreign graduates of the proposed school to enter special classes in these universities. The American and British Ambassadors, the Yokohama Foreign Board of Trade, and the President of the Bank of Japan have endorsed the enterprise in letters accompanying this Memorial.

Signed in behalf of the Committee.

Tokyo, July 10, 1912.

J. RUSSELL KENNEDY,
Chairman.

Members of the Special Committee:
  The British Ambassador,
  The American Ambassador,
    Honorary Members.
  D. C. Greene, LL.D., President, *ex officio*.
  J. Russell Kennedy, Chairman (Joint Treasurer) (Chief of Bureau of the Associated Press).
  J. Struthers, M.A., B.Sc., Joint Treasurer (Head of the Chilian Nitrate of Soda Propaganda of the Far East).
  D. H. Blake (Director of the American Trading Company).
  J. T. Swift, M.A. (Senior Professor of English, Tokyo Higher Normal School and Lecturer on the English Language in the Tokyo Imperial University).
  R. S. Miller (Chief of Bureau of the Far East, Department of State, Washington).
  T. F. Nonweiler (Director of the Japan Marine Insurance Company).

THE BOARD OF TRUSTEES.

The present Board of Trustees includes
  The Ambassadors of America and England.
  The Right Revd. Bishop Cecil of the English Church of Japan.
  The Right Revd. Bishop McKim, American Episcopal Bishop of Tokyo.
  The Right Revd. Bishop St. George Tucker, American Episcopal Bishop of Kyoto.
  The Right Revd. Bishop Harris, Methodist Bishop of Japan.

Automatically also, the leading representatives in Japan of the Mission Boards are members of the Board of Trustees.

The present school is entirely non-sectarian and cosmopolitan—a policy which it is hoped will be adopted by the directorate in every stage of the preparatory school in the Far East.

NOTE.

The accompanying documents are:
  Copies of letters from—
  1. The American Ambassador.
  2. The British Ambassador.
  3. The Governor of the Bank of Japan.
  4. The Chairman of the Foreign Board of Trade.
  5. Prof. Ernest D. Burton, of Chicago University.

Prospectus of the present Tokyo Grammar School for 1911-12.
Architect's blueprints of tentative plans for the buildings.
Report of Special Committee, 1911.
Report of Special Committee, 1912.
Letter from Mr. Struthers, the Treasurer, informally outlining his views.
Copy of *The Sumida,* a magazine issued by the school a few years ago.
Original estimates separately made by Mr. J. McD. Gardiner, the architect, **and by** Dr. D. Crosby Greene, the President.